YOUR TIME TO THRIVE

YOUR TIME TO *Thrive*

END BURNOUT, INCREASE WELL-BEING, AND UNLOCK YOUR FULL POTENTIAL WITH THE NEW SCIENCE OF MICROSTEPS

● ● ● ●

MARINA KHIDEKEL
AND THE EDITORS OF THRIVE GLOBAL

FOREWORD BY ARIANNA HUFFINGTON

hachette
BOOKS
NEW YORK

Hachette Go, an imprint of Hachette Books
Hachette Book Group
1290 Avenue of the Americas
New York, NY 10104
HachetteGo.com
Facebook.com/HachetteGo
Instagram.com/HachetteGo

First Paperback Edition: January 2023

Hachette Books is a division of Hachette Book Group, Inc.

The Hachette Go and Hachette Books names and logos are trademarks of Hachette Book Group, Inc.

The publisher is not responsible for websites (or their content) that are not owned by the publisher.

Print book interior design by Trish Wilkinson.

Library of Congress Cataloging-in-Publication Data

Names: Khidekel, Marina, author.
Title: Your time to thrive : end burnout, increase well-being, and unlock
    your full potential with the new science of microsteps / Marina Khidekel
    and the editors of Thrive Global ; foreword by Arianna Huffington.
Description: First edition. | New York, NY : Hachette Book Group, [2021] |
    Includes bibliographical references and index.
Identifiers: LCCN 2020046924 | ISBN 9780306875137 (hardcover) |
    ISBN 9780306847035 (hardcover) | ISBN 9780306847042 (hardcover) |
    ISBN 9780306875113 (ebook)
Subjects: LCSH: Stress (Psychology) | Burn out (Psychology) | Well-being. |
    Work-life balance.
Classification: LCC BF575.S75 K48 2021 | DDC 155.9/042—dc23
LC record available at https://lccn.loc.gov/2020046924

ISBNs: 978-0-306-87513-7 (hardcover), 978-0-306-87512-0 (trade paperback),
978-0-306-87511-3 (ebook), 978-0-306-84704-2 (signed edition),
978-0-306-84703-5 (B&N signed edition)

Printed in the United States of America

LSC-C

Printing 1, 2022

CONTENTS

FOREWORD

After my collapse from sleep deprivation and exhaustion in 2007, I became more and more passionate about the connection between well-being and performance. And as I went around the world speaking about my experience, I saw two things: First, that we're facing a stress and burnout epidemic. And second, that people deeply want to change the way they work and live.

That's why I launched Thrive Global—I wanted to go beyond raising awareness and create something real and tangible that would help individuals, companies, and communities improve their well-being and performance and unlock their greatest potential. (And debunk the collective delusion that burnout is the price we must pay for success.)

Thrive Global's mission is to end the epidemic of stress and burnout by changing the way we work and live. Yes, that's a big, ambitious goal, but there's a road map for us all to get there. To borrow from the famous coda of another long journey, it's less about giant leaps and more about small steps. We call these Microsteps, and they're at the heart of our behavior change system. Microsteps are small, science-backed actions we can start doing immediately to build healthy habits that significantly improve our lives.

Hold on *just* a second, you may say. The way to bring about significant, life-altering changes is through . . . small steps?

That's right. It's the idea that if you make the steps small enough, they'll be too small to fail. And the science is incontrovertible. At Thrive, we've taken this science and built a system that works for real people, helping them kickstart real change and start getting results—not weeks or months from now, but immediately.

Our science-backed approach has resonated with a multitude of audiences, from tech workers and new parents to call center workers and executives of multinational companies. We've created Microsteps to support mental health, showing people how to identify their individual signs of overstress and take action to recharge their mental batteries. This includes helping people deal with the stress and disruption of the COVID-19 pandemic with, you guessed it, Microsteps. We've created a series of Microsteps based on what neuroscientists call habit-stacking—attaching a new healthy habit to an existing habit to make it sustainable—for example, thinking of three things you're grateful for while brushing your teeth. And we've crafted Microsteps to include financial well-being, since financial stress isn't just about how much we have in our bank account but is connected to our overall well-being.

As people in every industry and at every level struggle to meet the demands of a fast-paced, hyperconnected world, Microsteps have emerged as an accessible solution empowering us to realize that the keys to changing our lives are at hand. And as the science makes clear, to improve our well-being, we don't need to turn our lives upside down and change everything about ourselves and how we live. Making even very small changes in our trajectory can, over time, lead us to a very different destination. By making our Microsteps too small to fail, we can make those first, small changes on which we can begin to build a new and healthier way of living and working. There's nothing wrong with aiming big—but we can help ourselves by starting small.

We've created an inspiring, motivational guide to incorporating Microsteps into your day-to-day activities—so you, too, can see success in every facet of your life. Led by Marina Khidekel, Thrive Global's head of content development, our team of editors (including Gregory Beyer, Margarita Bertsos, Alexandra Hayes Robinson, Elaine Lipworth, and Stephen Sherrill), together with Thrive's scientific advisers—neuroscientists, psychologists, and behavior change experts—weave together the science of Microsteps, ancient wisdom, real people's behavior change success stories, and of course, dozens of the most effective Microsteps. Whatever phase of life you're in, whatever your goals and circumstances, you'll find inspiration to take action. Think of it as your guidebook to a healthier, happier, more fulfilling life.

At Thrive, we take a whole human approach to behavior change. You'll find Microsteps that help you improve your physical health, build your mental resilience, strengthen your relationships with others, and experience the fulfillment that comes from being part of something larger than yourself. We've created this book with a focus on the pain points we see over and over again—the ones that most acutely prevent people from living the lives they want. These pain points might be holding you back too. What we also see again and again is that we can transform what's not working in our lives through small daily changes, which we'll help you implement throughout this book.

THE NEW SCIENCE OF MICROSTEPS

We are, as the saying goes, creatures of habit. According to a study from Duke University, around 45 percent of our everyday actions are made up of habits. Our habits, then, are a fundamental reflection of who we are. "Habit is but a long practice," Aristotle wrote, which "becomes men's nature in the end."

So our lifestyle is, in essence, the sum total of our habits. Change your habits and you change your life. But as most of us have learned, unlearning bad habits and learning new ones are not so easy. Even the most generous estimates show that half of us fail to keep our New Year's resolutions. That's because most of us start off too big. We decide to launch into a whole new lifestyle all at once. Or we think we're just going to get there by the sheer exercise of willpower. But that ignores the science of how willpower works. In their book *Willpower: Rediscovering the Greatest Human Strength*, Roy F. Baumeister, a leading expert in the subject, and coauthor John Tierney show that willpower isn't a fixed, genetic trait—it's a muscle, and one that can be strengthened.

And the best way to use our willpower to adopt healthier habits is by starting small. It's a common element of every successful behavior change program. "Make it easy" is how James Clear, author of *Atomic Habits: An Easy & Proven Way to Build Good Habits & Break Bad Ones*, puts it: "The central idea is to create an environment where doing the right thing is as easy as possible. Much of the battle of building better habits comes down to finding ways to reduce the friction associated with our good habits."

For BJ Fogg, director of the Behavior Design Lab at Stanford, it's about making the minimum viable effort—going as small as you can. "To create a new habit, you must first simplify the behavior," he says. "Make it tiny, even ridiculous. A good tiny behavior is easy to do—and fast."

The benefit of even one small win goes beyond just the new healthy behavior you've created—it actually builds that willpower muscle to create even more wins and good habits. "The more you succeed, the more capable you get at succeeding in the future," Fogg says. "So you don't start with the hardest behaviors first, you start with the ones you want to do and you can do and you persist."

In one of my favorite passages of Fogg's book *Tiny Habits: The Small Changes That Change Everything*, he shows how our tiny habits can spark a positive impact beyond just ourselves:

> Habits may be the smallest units of transformation, but they're also the most fundamental. They are the first concentric circles of change that will spiral out. Think about it. One person starts one habit that builds to two habits that builds to three habits that changes an identity that inspires a loved one who influences their peer group and changes their mindset, which spreads like wildfire and disrupts a culture of helplessness, empowering everyone and slowly changing the world. By starting small with yourself and your family, you set off a chain reaction that creates an explosion of change.

In my conversations with Fogg and Clear, I have been inspired by how they have pushed our understanding forward and helped establish the scientific foundation for the power of taking small steps. *Your Time to Thrive* builds on this foundation of behavior change, sharing a practical system for exactly how to implement Microsteps into each facet of our life. When it comes to leading a healthier, more fulfilling life, most of us know what we *should* do. And yet, all too often, we fail to act on this knowledge. We need a little help moving from knowing what to do to actually doing it. That's what our system is here for.

MORE ACTION, MORE MEANING

When we take Microsteps, we are not only moving forward, we're going inward. By creating rituals in our day, we allow ourselves to get into the metaphorical eye of the hurricane—that centered place of strength, wisdom, and peace that we all have inside ourselves. We all veer away from that place again and again—that's the nature of life. And it's a place that we are too distracted to access when we are living life breathlessly and always "on." But from that place we can tap into the inner reserves of resilience and wisdom that make behavior change possible.

Neuroscience shows, for example, that we can course-correct from stress in just sixty to ninety seconds. It's why one of my favorite Microsteps is focusing on the rising and falling of our breath, even for sixty seconds, which activates our parasympathetic nervous system, lowering our levels of the stress hormone cortisol.

This process ensures, in the simplest sense, that Microsteps work. But it doesn't just matter that they work—it also matters *how* they work. Creating meaningful, sustainable behavior change isn't just about helping people move from A to B in a mechanical way—getting in more steps every day, for instance, or managing our email inbox. It's about tapping into fundamental human needs and desires we all share—to live a better life, to unlock our greatest potential, to tap into what is best, wisest, and most creative and empathetic in us. In other words, tapping into our *heart*.

So you'll find this heart—heartfulness? heart-itude?—generously sprinkled throughout the book. It's there in the stories of people committed to improving themselves. It's in the notes of ancient wisdom woven throughout the book, connecting us to timeless truths. And it's in the Microsteps themselves. You can see it in this Microstep, which happens to be one of my favorites:

Pick a time at night when you turn off your devices—and gently escort them out of your bedroom. Our phones are repositories of everything we need to put away to allow us to sleep—our to-do lists, our inboxes, multiple projects, and problems. Disconnecting from the digital world will help you sleep better, deeply recharge, and reconnect to your wisdom and creativity.

It's one of my favorites because, for me, it is impossible to separate this Microstep from a very specific moment in my life—a moment when behavior change wasn't just something I aspired to, but something I desperately needed.

On April 6, 2007, I woke up in a pool of my own blood. I was two years into building the Huffington Post. A divorced mother of two teenage daughters, I had just returned from a week of taking my eldest daughter on a tour of prospective colleges. And since she had insisted that I not use my Blackberry during the day (the Blackberry, if you're not familiar, was a communication device used in ancient times), I would stay up each night working. And so, the morning after we returned home, I woke up burned out and exhausted—and then I collapsed. The result was a broken cheekbone, several stitches over my eye, and the beginning of a long journey.

In the days that followed, I found myself in a lot of doctors' waiting rooms, which, it turns out, are great places to think about life. And that's what I did. I asked myself a lot of questions, like *Is this what success really looks like? Is this the life I want to lead?*

The answer was no. And the diagnosis I got from all the doctors was that I had a severe case of burnout. So I decided to make a lot of changes to my life. I started meditating again, which I had learned to do as a child. I changed the way I worked so I could be more productive, more focused, more energetic, and less tired and stressed. I started sleeping more. I knew my sleep deprivation was directly connected to my addiction to my phone—it *was* an addiction—and to my flawed definition of success. I got deep into the growing body of science on the connection between well-being and performance, and how we can actually be more productive when we prioritize our well-being and take time to unplug and recharge. And—eureka!—a Microstep was born.

My seventieth birthday, in July 2020, was a powerful reminder to me that we don't need to wait to begin living our best life. At the time I was sheltering in place with my daughters and sister at our family home in LA, and while cleaning out the garage I came across dozens of old journals and notebooks filled with pages and pages of my thoughts and goals and worries and dreams from my twenties on!

And as I read back through half a century of notes, I was struck by four things. First, by how early I knew what really mattered in life. Second, how badly I was at acting on that knowledge. Third, how draining and depleting all my worries and fears were. And fourth, how little those worries and fears turned out to matter.

As I paged through my old notebooks, I wanted to shout advice at myself across the years—telling the younger me not to worry or doubt so much, or to just go ahead and take that risk. And that is one of my biggest hopes for this book: that instead of looking at those fearless and wise elders among us and thinking, "I want to be that way when I'm old," we can use Microsteps to tap into what is wisest, boldest, and most authentic within us and live each day from that place right now, however young or old we may be.

HOW YOU CAN THRIVE

This book explores many aspects of the way we work and live in our modern world, but it's really about one thing: giving you the tools and support you need to change your life for the better. Our system begins with foundational aspects of well-being, starting with sleep, and builds to address topics that deepen our understanding of what it means to live a thriving life—both for ourselves and in connection with others. There's a reason why airline attendants always instruct us that, in the case of emergency, we'll be most able to help others if we secure our own oxygen masks first. Not because we're selfish, but because that is how we're going to be at our best and most effective.

Another thing the science tells us: a successful behavior change journey begins with a mindset shift. Think of your mindset as the story you tell yourself—about yourself. If you think of yourself as someone who can't or won't improve your life, it's time to shift that belief. If past attempts at behavior change have failed or stalled, no matter. By starting with just one Microstep—and perhaps habit-stacking it on top of something you already do every day—you'll build a foundation for positive change. Armed with the science in these pages and inspired by ancient wisdom and the stories of others who have discovered the life-changing power of Microsteps, you'll be on your way to making small changes that lead to big results—immediately.

So pick an area you want to focus on and commit to a Microstep—just one!—that resonates with you. If you miss a day here and there or veer off course, don't judge yourself. Simply start again. And remember, you have the power to change your life—one Microstep at a time.

—*Arianna Huffington, founder and CEO, Thrive Global*

INTRODUCTION

• • • •

THE CASE FOR TAKING SMALL STEPS IN OVERWHELMING TIMES (OR, WHY SHOULD YOU BOTHER WITH THIS BOOK?)

As I worked with Thrive Global's editors to bring this book to life, we had a guiding principle, which became a refrain: there's nothing wrong with aiming big, but we can help ourselves by starting small.

That was true when we started writing *Your Time to Thrive*, when we were already facing an epidemic of stress and burnout. And it became *really* true when COVID-19 hit. In a world reshaped by the pandemic, so many of us are simply trying to stay physically and mentally healthy and be the best people, partners, and parents we can be in a historically difficult time. The idea of making big, dramatic life changes doesn't just feel hopelessly daunting. It's unrealistic. Maybe even ridiculous.

That's why this book is all about small, incremental mindset and behavior shifts. It's why the unit of change at the heart of our approach is the Microstep, not the giant leap. And it's why we've created a science-backed behavior change system that helps you move from merely surviving to thriving.

Only it doesn't feel like a system. (We're sneaky like that.) *Your Time to Thrive* is broken down into small, manageable actions you can adapt to your life in ways that work for you. There's a reason we say they're "too small to fail": the science shows that it's precisely these tiny steps that help us build habits, which over time lead to big, meaningful improvements in our lives.

As you begin to explore the Microsteps within these pages, you may think to yourself, "These don't seem like such a big deal." Correct! That's exactly the idea. With minimal time and effort, you can seamlessly integrate Microsteps into your days, with immediate benefits for your well-being, resilience, focus, relationships, and sense of purpose. And over time, the results can add up to a very big deal indeed.

That's what happened with my own favorite Microstep. Like most of us, I would start my mornings by checking my phone as soon as I woke up. I never liked the feeling I got when I did this, but when the pandemic hit, I realized I was experiencing a palpable spike of anxiety each morning—a shortness of breath that took hours to go away. So I vowed to try the Microstep of not checking my phone for at least one minute after waking. Instead I decided I would first take a few deep breaths and set my intentions for the day. I would sometimes even wait until I'd taken a shower to unlock my phone.

Breaking my old habit took a few tries, but I stuck with it, and this tiny shift made a huge impact on my stress levels. I had known that checking my phone before even brushing my teeth wasn't a good idea, but until I stopped doing it, I didn't realize *why* it was so bad. When you check your phone first thing, what you're doing is starting your day focused on what other people expect from you (email, Slack threads, texts), what others prioritize in their lives (social media), and all the instability going on in the world (headlines) instead of focusing on what *you* want from your day. Since incorporating this change into my mornings, I've realized the value of taking a couple minutes (and sometimes a hot shower) for ourselves, and letting our thoughts assemble themselves before turning our attention to the outside world. In fact, those quiet moments have become a calm respite for me (no more daily anxiety spike), and have even created an opening for some creative ideas to bubble to the surface. And the benefits carry over into the rest of my day, in the way I interact with others and what I choose to prioritize.

Of course, I'm far from alone in seeing the impact a single Microstep can have. At Thrive, we don't just create Microsteps and share them with the world, we practice them in our own lives. (We also have a big, colorful Microstep wall in our New York office, complete with magnetic Microstep stickers that visitors can choose and take home with them for inspiration!) Throughout the book, we share the stories of many of our Thrive colleagues as they challenged themselves to test a Microstep for thirty-two days. The resulting Microstep Diaries are honest and encouraging, and they will give you a sense of how Microsteps can fit into a busy life. At the end of each chapter you'll find a page where you can take a moment to think about how to incorporate those Microsteps into your own life.

There's just one more thing I want to add before you dive into the book. It's become clear that one key value we need to prioritize if we are to thrive in our Next Normal is compassion—both for others and for ourselves. The practice of Microsteps isn't meant to be a sink-or-swim proposition. It's a journey, and one that you really can't get wrong. If you start working on a Microstep and fall off the wagon (or decide you'd rather prioritize a different one), that is more than okay. This idea of self-compassion came into sharp relief for me during the making of this book. As I was working on the chapter about focus and prioritization, I found myself attempting to multitask—check emails, reply to Slacks, prep for my next Zoom meeting—no fewer than ten times. The irony wasn't lost on me that as I was editing a section about how multitasking helps *no one*, there I was trying to do it anyway. And of course, meanwhile, I was failing miserably in being productive or creative. I finally made myself stop everything, took a few deep breaths, blocked off twenty minutes of "heads-down" time on my calendar, and came back to the work. I wanted to practice what we preached, but I also wanted to stop mentally punishing myself when I stumbled. Any time my mind wandered after that, I would do the "block off a small chunk of focused time" Microstep again. It took a few tries (and I was kinder to myself on subsequent slipups), but I'm happy to report I've made it a habit.

The point is, we can do this! And I'm so excited to go on this journey with you. As you begin to make small changes in the areas of life that matter most to you, you'll see—as I did—just how powerful Microsteps can be.

—*Marina Khidekel,*
Thrive Global's head of content development

1
● ● ●

SLEEP

*I*f we're going to truly thrive, we must begin with sleep. It is one of humanity's great unifiers. It binds us to one another, to our ancestors, to our past, and to the future. No matter who we are or where we are in the world and in our lives, we share a common need for sleep. But in our fast-paced, hyperconnected world, a good night's sleep has never been harder to come by.

As I shared in the Foreword, for much of my life I bought into a definition of success marked by sleep deprivation, exhaustion, and a frenetic, breathless way of living. It worked well for me—until it didn't. But after my painful wake-up call, I began to rekindle my relationship with sleep. Getting seven or eight hours of sleep became a nonnegotiable for me, and Microsteps helped me get there. The benefits were immediately apparent. Not only did I wake up feeling refreshed, it became easier to meditate and exercise, make wiser decisions, and connect more deeply with myself and others.

Now I get asked all the time how much sleep I get. That's what happens when you write a book called The Sleep Revolution, *travel around the world talking about it, and found a company committed to ending our global burnout crisis. So when the question comes, I'm ready: I reply that 95 percent of the time I get eight hours per night.*

What about the other 5 percent? When I don't get the sleep I need, I instead get a glimpse of my old life of burnout, feeling exhausted and underslept, and begging for a third Starbucks to stay awake. Every now and then lack of sleep happens, and I get irritable, my mind is cloudy, I'm looking for toothpicks to keep my eyes open, and there isn't a lot of joy in what I'm doing.

That's how I know that maintaining my eight hours habit is well worth it. And why I've repeatedly renewed my vows in my love affair with sleep.

I learned the hard way what happens when I don't get sufficient sleep. Here we share the latest science, role models, and actionable Microsteps to help you get the sleep you need—so you can be your best, most rested, most fulfilled self. Whatever your current relationship with sleep, you'll find inspiration and advice to make immediate changes and improve every aspect of your life.

—Arianna Huffington

● ● ●

WHILE EVERY TOPIC covered in this book is essential, with potential to improve key aspects of our lives, there is one that lies at the core of the connection between our well-being and performance: sleep.

Sleep is like a gateway—or, as some experts call it, a "keystone habit." "Keystone habits start a process that, over time, transforms everything," writes Charles Duhigg, author of *The Power of Habit*. "Keystone habits say that success doesn't depend on getting every single thing right, but instead relies on identifying a few key priorities and fashioning them into powerful levers."

When we think of sleep as a luxury we can't afford, we pay a price—in terms of our physical and mental health, relationships, performance, focus, and more. But when we make sleep a priority, it becomes a powerful lever, making other important habits and decisions easier. In fact, getting even just a little more sleep enhances your ability to make meaningful changes in all the areas we explore throughout this book.

Of course, when it comes to making sleep a priority, we're up against some harsh realities: the accelerated pace and "always on" nature of modern life. Our modern society's definition of success, which tells us that sleep is idle or even wasted time. And perhaps most of all, the delusion that we can either get the sleep we need or we can succeed at work—but we can't do both.

We can't undo or even ignore these realities. But as we'll see, we can make small changes in our routines that allow us to get the sleep we need—with big, immediate results for the rest of our lives.

ENDING OUR COLLECTIVE DELUSION

Throughout history, until our modern era, sleep was respected and even revered. Sleep and dreams have played a singular role in virtually every religion and spiritual tradition. The Greeks and the Romans each had their gods of sleep: Hypnos for the Greeks, Somnus for the Romans.

But somewhere along the line, our culture began to devalue sleep. As Thich Nhat Hanh, the renowned Vietnamese Buddhist monk, says, "We humans have lost the wisdom of genuinely resting and relaxing. We worry too much. We don't allow our bodies to heal, and we don't allow our minds and hearts to heal." We're only now beginning to come out of a phase that started with the Industrial Revolution, in which sleep became just another obstacle to work.

Consider some of the ways this attitude still shapes our relationship with sleep. All too often, we associate sleep with a lack of ambition or commitment, or consider it a luxury we simply can't afford. We brag about how little sleep we get, and we celebrate others for pulling all-nighters or burning the candle at both ends. Much of our society is still operating under the collective delusion that sleep is simply time lost to other pursuits, that sleep can be endlessly appropriated to satisfy our fast-paced lives and over-stuffed to-do lists—a delusion perfectly captured in the phrase "I'll sleep when I'm dead."

For those who believe they can operate at peak levels without sufficient sleep, the justification usually goes something like this: "Sure, other people need a full night's sleep in order to function and be healthy and alert. But I'm different." The truth, however, is that less than 1 percent of the population actually qualifies as "short sleepers"—those rare few who are able to get by on little sleep without experiencing negative

---

HOW I THRIVE

TIFFANY CRUIKSHANK, bestselling author and founder of Yoga Medicine

Turn down the lights in your home when it's nearing bedtime.

"A couple hours before bed, I start to slow down, power down, and turn the lights down to help slowly lower my cortisol. I'm very protective of this sleep ritual, no matter where I am in the world."

━ ● ● ● ━

YOUR BRAIN ON SLEEP

Sleep is a period of extraordinary and meaningful activity for the brain. Recently, researchers have even discovered that sleep acts as a sort of "flushing out" system for the brain, clearing out harmful waste proteins that build up between its cells—a process that may reduce the risk of Alzheimer's and other brain diseases. . . .

How many hours of sleep do we need? There are indeed individual differences, but the rough rule of thumb is to get five sleep cycles of 90 minutes each, which translates to 7.5 hours of sleep.

So if you want to make better decisions, rise to a higher level of performance, and take care of your brain, commit to getting the sleep you need, every night. Your morning self—recharged, refreshed, and ready to take on the biggest challenges and most important decisions—will thank you.

—Baba Shiv, professor of marketing, Stanford Graduate School
of Business, who has done extensive work on the emotional
brain and its role in shaping decisions and experiences

consequences. (Though many people would like to believe they can train themselves to gain admission to the short-sleeping 1 percent, the trait is actually the result of a genetic mutation.)

And yet modern science is validating ancient wisdom around the value of sleep. Study after study affirms sleep's benefits to our well-being, performance, and ability to live a more fulfilling life. Sleep is an essential period of recovery for the body and brain, and it facilitates memory, learning, repair, productivity, emotional intelligence, mood, creativity, and resilience.

Just look at what happens in the brain while we sleep. We may imagine sleep to be a period of idleness, but in reality it's a time of incredible activity. It's like bringing in an overnight cleaning crew to clear the toxic waste proteins that accumulate between brain cells. Maiken Nedergaard, a neuroscientist at the University of Rochester Medical Center, says sleep is "like a dishwasher" for the brain. As Heraclitus, the ancient Greek philosopher, wrote, "Even a soul submerged in sleep is hard at work and helps make something of the world."

When we deny our brain this time to clean and recharge, we pay a price. In fact, skimping on sleep has shown similar effects to being intoxicated. For many of us, being awake for seventeen to nineteen hours is a normal day. But when we're awake this long we can experience levels of cognitive impairment equal to having a blood alcohol level just under the legal limit in many US states. And if we're awake just a few hours more, we're up to the equivalent of being legally intoxicated.

And while we may feel accomplished and productive when burning the midnight oil, we also know that when we're sleep deprived, we're simply less likely to be the best version of ourselves. This can have consequences not only for our poor, exhausted selves, but for anyone unlucky enough to come into contact with us. A study from Karolinska Institutet in Stockholm, Sweden, found that even one night of bad sleep can mess up our mood and challenge our ability to regulate our emotions, which can strain even our social interactions.

SETTING THE SCENE FOR SLEEP

Sleep doesn't exist in a vacuum (unless you're Michael Phelps, the champion swimmer who retires each night in a low-oxygen, high-altitude sleep chamber). Our ability to get the sleep we need depends heavily on environmental factors. As nice as it sounds, most of us aren't able to simply fall into restorative sleep the second our head hits the pillow at the end of a demanding and fast-paced day. But if we put just a bit of forethought and effort into creating a more welcoming sleep environment, the outcomes can be transformative.

Let's start with the bedroom. Personal preferences vary, but research has given us clear guidelines on how to create conditions in our bedroom that will ease our transition to sleep. With Microsteps, we can make small changes to our environment that can yield big results. As Arianna wrote in *The Sleep Revolution*, "When we walk through the door of our bedroom, it should be a symbolic moment that marks leaving the day, with all of its problems and unfinished business, behind us."

We can start by banishing our phones from our bedroom at a certain time each night. Our phones are repositories of everything we need to put away to allow us to sleep—our to-do lists, our inboxes, multiple projects, and problems. Plus, the blue light given off by our electronic devices suppresses melatonin, which make these devices especially bad for our sleep. According to George Brainard, a circadian rhythm researcher and neurologist at Thomas Jefferson University in Philadelphia, staring at a blue-light-emitting device before bed serves as "an alert stimulus that will frustrate your body's ability to go to sleep later." For those of us who like to end the day with an episode (or four) of our favorite show, it's worth knowing how this habit can eat into our sleep. For American adults, 88 percent admit they have lost sleep because of binge-watching shows, according to a recent survey from the American Academy of Sleep Medicine.

Then there's the temperature of your bedroom. We know that being too hot or too cold can get in the way of a good night's sleep. And, in fact, there are clear guidelines: the National Sleep Foundation recommends sixty-five degrees and says that sleep is disrupted when the temperature rises above seventy-five degrees or falls below fifty-four degrees.

Just as sleep, as a keystone habit, impacts other parts of our lives, our choices leading up to bedtime affect our sleep—even those activities we might not associate with sleep. For example, it's true that eating big meals right before bed isn't a great idea. Late-night snacking or turning to food to power through a late-night work session can backfire. "We have this illusion that with the flip of a switch, we can work at any time and part of that is eating at any time," said Christopher Colwell, a professor of psychiatry at UCLA. "But our biological systems . . . work based on having a daily rhythm."

HOW I THRIVE

TOM BRADY, NFL quarterback and Super Bowl champion

Turn off all your electronic devices a half hour before you go to sleep.

"If there's a TV in your bedroom, consider putting it somewhere else. It's a bedroom, not a tech cave. My wife doesn't even allow cell phones near the bed when we sleep."

● ● ●

The way our modern lives are organized makes this hard. It *does* feel like we are flipping a switch from on mode to off mode, trading the demands of the day for however many hours of sleep we can squeeze in. But with Microsteps we can create bedtime rituals that ease the transition, reduce our stress, and even bring more pleasure to each evening. Taking a bath or shower, sipping chamomile or lavender tea, even putting on pajamas can serve as a symbolic moment when we pass from the arena of action into the realm of recharging.

These rituals serve a dual purpose, not only preparing us for sleep but helping us to leave the day—with its stresses, worries, and to-do lists—behind us. As Ralph Waldo Emerson put it, "Finish every day, and be done with it. . . . You have done what you could—some blunders and absurdities no doubt crept in, forget them as fast as you can, tomorrow is a new day. You shall begin it well and serenely, and with too high a spirit to be encumbered with your old nonsense."

HOW I THRIVE

TAMRON HALL, broadcast journalist and talk show host

Take a midday nap.

"My days are split between very early mornings and evening events, so I really try to energize with afternoon naps. But never longer than 30 to 35 minutes; anything longer than that is a problem."

GOOD SLEEP STARTS EARLIER THAN WE THINK

Naturally, we associate sleep with the nighttime. But one mindset shift we can make that will improve our ability to sleep when nighttime comes around is to identify Microsteps we can take throughout the day.

When we devote small moments throughout the day to re-charging, we create pockets of meaning and connection we may have been missing—without even knowing we were missing them. And it's not just about shut-eye; it's about enhancing the quality of every moment we're awake.

"Over the course of the day, little stressors cumulatively have a pretty big impact on our resting physiological tension," Simon Rego, chief psychologist at the Albert Einstein College of Medicine's Montefiore Medical Center in New York City, tells Thrive. He likens our daily doses of stress—getting the kids ready for school, rush hour traffic, work pressures, smart-phone notifications—to a pot of water on the stove that reaches a boiling point by the end of the day.

So while sleep might be the last thing on our mind when we're starting the day, we have an opportunity to set ourselves up for success from the moment we wake up. For example, get-ting exercise throughout the day helps—and it doesn't have to mean going to the gym. University of Pennsylvania researchers showed that those who walked for exercise got better sleep and that, as lead author Michael Grandner put it, "these effects are even stronger for more purposeful activities, such as running and yoga, and even gardening and golf." Small changes in the course of a busy day, such as taking the stairs instead of the elevator, are sneakily effective.

Many of us depend on caffeine to help us power through our days. There's nothing wrong with that, as long as we know when to cut ourselves off, since too much caffeine hinders our ability to sleep at night. We should be aware of how caffeine

> ● ● ● ●

WE NO LONGER HAVE TO ASK WHAT SLEEP IS GOOD FOR

The physical and mental impairments caused by one night of bad sleep dwarf those caused by an equivalent absence of food or exercise. It is difficult to imagine any other state—natural or medically manipulated—that affords a more powerful redressing of physical and mental health at every level of analysis.

Based on a rich, new scientific understanding of sleep, we no longer have to ask what sleep is good for. Instead, we are now forced to wonder whether there are any biological functions that do *not* benefit by a good night's sleep. So far, the results of thousands of studies insist that no, there aren't.

—Matthew Walker, PhD, professor of neuroscience and
psychology at the University of California, Berkeley,
and author of *Why We Sleep*

affects us personally, but also know that caffeine has a half-life of five to six hours. Many experts recommend not consuming caffeinated beverages after 2 p.m.

If we're not getting the seven or eight hours a night of sleep we need, researchers have found that even short naps can help us course-correct. According to David Randall, author of *Dreamland: Adventures in the Strange Science of Sleep*, a short nap "primes our brains to function at a higher level, letting us come up with better ideas, find solutions to puzzles more quickly, identify patterns faster and recall information more accurately."

And if you've come to equate napping with laziness or a lack of ambition, consider that, throughout history, famous nappers have included Leonardo da Vinci, Eleanor Roosevelt, Thomas Edison, Winston Churchill, and John F. Kennedy. More recent nap champions include marketing executive Bozoma Saint John, TV host Andy Cohen, NBA star Steph Curry, and Olympic marathoner Ryan Hall.

SLEEP'S GREAT AWAKENING

As study after study affirms the science-backed connection between sleep and performance, more and more results-driven leaders in every profession are talking about sleep as a superpower—and showing others how to take action through Microsteps. That's because they've realized sleep's direct connection to decision-making, productivity, and other measures of success.

Jeff Bezos told Thrive that eight hours of sleep a night makes a big difference for him, so he tries hard to make it a priority. "If you shortchange your sleep, you might get a couple of extra 'productive' hours, but that productivity might be an illusion," he said. "When you're talking about

---

HOW I THRIVE

HODA KOTB, co-anchor of the *TODAY* show and *TODAY with Hoda & Jenna*

Before bed, read a few pages from an inspiring book.

"I try to fill the last couple of minutes before I close my eyes with something nourishing, whether it's a book I keep on my bedside table, or something that I read that's uplifting."

• • •

decisions and interactions, quality is usually more important than quantity." And as Kristin Lemkau, chief marketing officer for JPMorgan Chase, put it, "Sleep loss deteriorates judgment. When I look back on mistakes I've made—hiring the wrong person, approving something that needed more work, or snapping at someone who didn't deserve it—they all have one thing in common. I was tired. When I'm tired, I put off tough conversations. And when I'm tired, I'm not the leader, the mother, or the person I strive to be. *Everything* suffers."

And while the world of tech startups is practically synonymous with burnout and sleep deprivation, that's changing. Reid Hoffman, a venture capitalist and cofounder of LinkedIn, describes the myth of the burned-out entrepreneur as a "pervasive tale that you can—and that you must—work inhumanly long hours. Put yourself under enormous stress. Forego sleep, meals, relationships and life's other pleasures. And that doing so is a fundamental part of the founder's journey. Taking too many gulps of this particularly popular flavor of Kool-Aid is a path paved with peril."

Those who equate sleep with laziness or lack of dedication may want to consider what's going on in the world of sports. To professional athletes, sleep is all about performance. It's about what works, about using every available tool to increase the chances of winning.

Olympic gold medalist Mikaela Shiffrin's daily routine includes a heavy focus on sleep. In fact, the skier is known for her sleep schedule. In addition to logging an average of nine hours per night, she "is famous for her naps—she requires an hour a day, and has been known to snooze in the snow in the starting area of a race," according to the *New Yorker*.

Then there's NBA all-star Andre Iguodala. At the height of his career, he made sleep a priority. But it wasn't always that way. He'd stay up late watching TV and then hit the gym early. On game days he'd take three- or four-hour naps, but his performance suffered. Sleep turned out to be the key piece that was missing from his routine.

With the help of a sleep therapist he began to make small changes. When Iguodala adjusted to a consistent eight hours of sleep a night, his points per minute went up 29 percent, his free-throw percentage increased 8.9 percent, his three-point-shot percentages more than doubled. Meanwhile, his turnovers decreased 37 percent and fouls dropped 45 percent.

Sure, Iguodala had the help of a top-notch sleep therapist (Cheri Mah, MS, MD, one of the most sought-after sleep scientists in the sports world). But the steps he took were modest. "My pre-bed routine is pretty much shutting down all the phones, putting everything on airplane mode and then I'm just kind of decompressing,

---

HOW I THRIVE

SHELLY IBACH, CEO of Sleep Number and Thrive Global's sleep editor-at-large

When you can't fall asleep, breathe deeply and think about what you're grateful for.

"Lying awake in bed and mulling over your to-do list can be distressing. Personally, when I wake up too early, I breathe deeply and slowly and take those predawn moments to relax and think about what I am grateful for. . . . Try closing your eyes and placing your attention on joyful, calming thoughts, whether that's family, friends, pets, nature, or a favorite vacation spot."

• • • •

forgetting about everything—no screens, no lights, making sure the temperature's right in the bedroom and then I'm ready to go. When I get enough sleep I'm just in a better mood."

Even if we're not leading companies or competing for NBA titles, we have an opportunity to bring about real improvements in our work and life, just by giving sleep the respect it deserves. Whatever challenge we're facing, whatever accomplishment we're aiming for, we can remember the words of John Steinbeck, who wrote, "It is a common experience that a problem difficult at night is resolved in the morning after the committee of sleep has worked on it."

As we discussed at the beginning of this chapter, sleep is the ultimate keystone habit. When we are our rested, recharged selves, we are in the strongest position to build and sustain the habits we'll explore in the chapters to come—habits that allow us to truly thrive.

●　●　●

MICROSTEP DIARY

At Thrive, we're always challenging ourselves to build healthy new habits with Microsteps. Here, marketing manager of product and brand Clarice Metzger shares her story.

MICROSTEP: Set an alarm for thirty minutes before your bedtime

Why I Chose It

I wanted to start establishing a bedtime routine and use the thirty minutes to unwind before bed. Even if my routine is just making sure that I'm not doing work right until I close my eyes and fall asleep.

What Happened

I consistently practiced my Microstep—the alarm went off every night—but I usually did not end up going to sleep within those thirty minutes. Sometimes I'd be in the middle of something, and wouldn't finish up in those thirty minutes.

When I did actually do a thirty-minute wind-down routine—shower, drink tea, and do a face mask—I felt accomplished and relaxed, so that as soon as I lay in bed, I fell asleep. When I didn't, I found myself in bed scrolling through Instagram, unable to fall asleep right away.

I wouldn't call this Microstep a habit *yet*, but it's something I'm continuing to work on in order to make it a habit. My main learning is that I need to get home earlier in order to have time to unwind. If I could do one thing differently, it would be to get home earlier so that I can make dinner and prepare myself for the next day, so that I don't feel as though I have so much left to do before winding down. I'm going to try that strategy moving forward, so I can set the alarm and actually stick to it!

MICROSTEPS

Before bed, escort your devices out of your bedroom. Disconnecting from the digital world will help you sleep better, deeply recharge, and reconnect to your wisdom and creativity.

Set an alarm for thirty minutes before your bedtime. Setting an alarm reminds you that if you're going to get to bed on time, you need to start wrapping things up.

Set a daily caffeine cutoff. Taken too late in the day, caffeine hinders our ability to fall asleep. Switch to decaf after 2 p.m.—your nighttime self will thank you.

Conduct a sleep audit. Spend time identifying where on the spectrum your sleep quality and quantity might fall, and what beliefs, behaviors, and mindsets might be driving your sleep habits. Taking the time to list them out might create new awareness and ideas so that you can implement the Microsteps you need to get better sleep.

Rid your bedroom of unwanted noise. Sound is one of the simplest and most direct impediments to deep sleep. Identify any sources of unwanted noise (starting with your devices) and either remove them from your bedroom or silence them.

Set a news cutoff time at the end of the day. While being informed can help us feel more prepared amid a public health crisis, for example, setting healthy limits to our media consumption can help us have a recharging night's sleep and put stressful news into perspective.

Keep your bedroom cool (between sixty-five and sixty-nine degrees). Set your thermostat to your preferred cool temperature. Research shows even a small drop in our body temperature sends a sleep signal to our brains.

Wear dedicated sleepwear to bed. When you get dressed for sleep, whether it's in pajamas or a special T-shirt, it sends a sleep-friendly message to your body.

Sip chamomile or lavender tea to ease yourself into sleep mode. Drinking something warm and comforting can put you in a calm frame of mind and help you shed your stubborn daytime worries.

Ease yourself into sleep by meditating in bed. Even a few deep breaths will help ease your transition to sleep. If you don't meditate, try playing a guided sleep meditation on your iPod or similar device.

Before you go to sleep, take sixty seconds to write down a list of three things you need to do tomorrow. Research shows that writing down your key priorities can help you fall asleep faster than reflecting on completed activities or things that already happened. Refer back to your list in the morning and dive in!

HOW YOU CAN THRIVE

What are some of the biggest challenges you face that keep you from getting the sleep you need?

What environmental factors make it harder for you to sleep?

What are some limiting beliefs you have around sleep or sleep messages that have stuck with you? For example: *Other people need a full night's sleep to function and perform at their best, but I'm different* or *I'll sleep when I'm dead.*

Did any of the science or stories in this chapter help you think differently about the connection between sleep, well-being, and performance?

What's one sleep Microstep you read that you can try tonight?

Consider these tips for really making your sleep Microsteps and goals stick:

- Choose an accountability partner to check in with
- Add your Microstep to your calendar
- Habit-stack your Microstep onto an existing habit or ritual

2

• • • •

UNPLUGGING
AND RECHARGING

*T*echnology *is great at giving us what we think we want, but it's not necessarily great at giving us what we need. If you've ever spent an evening mindlessly scrolling through social media before bed, or struggling to get through a meeting or a meal without checking your phone, you know what I mean.*

Our relationship with technology is the ultimate paradox: the same devices that create opportunities for connection and convenience also sap our time and attention. It's a relationship that impacts other key aspects of our well-being and performance, from our sleep and mental health to our ability to focus and authentically connect with others.

If someone was ringing your doorbell and summoning you to your front door every two seconds, you'd probably disconnect your doorbell. Or move to another house. But most people are still remarkably open about allowing their attention and their time—which is some very valuable real estate—to be summoned by others via their devices.

Most of us, myself included, need a little help creating new norms about how we use technology—to go from valuing always being on

*to also valuing unplugging and recharging. We don't need to re-
nounce technology—not at all. But we can realize what we're really missing out on when we give into the conventional notion of
FOMO (fear of missing out), and take Microsteps to set healthy
boundaries.*

*One of my favorite Microsteps, which became especially helpful
as the reality of life during lockdown sank in, is this: Set a news
and social media cut-off time. While being informed can help us
feel more prepared, setting healthy limits to our media consumption can help us have a recharging sleep and put stressful news into
perspective.*

—Arianna Huffington

• • • •

AFTER RACKING UP over a billion views and producing nearly
four hundred videos, YouTube's original beauty star Michelle
Phan shocked her fans and followers in 2015 by leaving the
platform. The reason? Her rise to top influencer status had come
at a big cost: Phan was burned out and needed a break. "I like
to make this comparison that being a YouTuber is like being
an Uber driver, and your car is your channel," she tells Thrive.
"Uber drivers are not going to make money unless they're driving that car. Essentially, that's the same as a YouTuber. You
have to make content on a pretty consistent daily basis because
people in the audience, they love seeing new content every
week, or every day. That's why the burnout rate is so high."

So after ten years of pushing hard on the gas pedal, Phan
took a two-year YouTube hiatus. The very devices that fueled her livelihood eventually delivered the warning signs that

something was amiss. "You know you have a problem when you hear your phone vibrate and you start feeling stressed out. That's when you realize, 'Okay, I have a problem,'" Phan recalls. "I was tired, I wasn't creating anything I was proud of, and that was why I took a break . . . to take a few steps back and reflect."

Phan's story represents a problem that many of us—across every industry—also face: an inability to find our "off" switch. Even if we know how important it is to regularly unplug from technology and recharge our own batteries, the architecture of our modern lives doesn't make it easy. We love our phones, our screens, our devices and what they allow us to do. We value the convenience and connection they've brought to modern life. But having the world at our fingertips, and in our pockets, has accelerated the pace of our lives unlike ever before. And it's brought a whole new universe of temptations, notifications, and alerts that often make it seem like we're living in service of our devices rather than leveraging their tools to make our lives better. If we struggled to set boundaries before, the COVID-19 pandemic has only heightened the challenge; if we thought working from home would make it easier to disconnect from email and all the apps that connect us to the stress of our workdays, well, we were wrong.

To understand just how dependent many of us have become on our devices, consider an experiment conducted by researchers at Harvard and the University of Virginia. They gave people a choice to be alone in a room, without anything—no devices, no papers, no phones—or get an electric shock. A whopping 67 percent of men and 25 percent of women chose the electric shock.

If you're accustomed to dashing off late-night work emails, or if you're one of the 86 percent of Americans who check email, texts, and social media constantly or often, you know: our relationship with technology makes it especially hard for us to declare an end to our workday.

Consider the case of Elon Musk, the visionary founder and CEO of Tesla. In November 2018, Musk tweeted that "nobody ever changed the world on 40 hours a week." But speaking to the *New York Times* about his 120-hour workweeks, he was frank about the cost of his always-on existence: "There were times when I didn't leave the factory for three or four days—days when I didn't go outside. This has really come at the expense of seeing my kids. And seeing friends."

This way of working and living isn't just a Silicon Valley phenomenon. As Claire Cain Miller writes in the *New York Times*, "Overwork (or at least time in the office or online, regardless of whether much work is getting done) has become increasingly common in more jobs," including "any job in which someone's manager stays late or sends emails on weekends and expects employees to follow suit." Thanks to

---

HOW I THRIVE

DEMI MOORE, actress

Do a one-minute meditation before getting out of bed.

"Before I pick up any of my devices (because once you pick them up you can be sucked down the rabbit hole), it's my time to meditate and set my intentions for the day."

A SIMPLE NEW RULE FOR BEING PRESENT

A few years ago, I had a little epiphany at home. It was a gorgeous morning and I wanted to take my three kids to the playground. They were up for the trip, they said, but asked if our brand-new babysitter at that time could take them instead . . . because they knew I would just spend the whole time on my phone. My family is the most important thing in the world to me. And they got me thinking about what it means to balance it all in a high-intensity world: the demands of work and life in our always-on age. . . . I realized there was no point blocking off time for family if I wasn't really present. So I made a new simple rule and told my kids right away: When they're around, I can't be on my phone . . . and trust me, they hold me to it.

—Philipp Schindler, Google's chief business officer

technology, workers are more reachable than ever. When it's so easy to stay connected, even sick days—which in theory should involve no work and be dedicated to rest and recovery—have a way of becoming sick-but-I'll-be-online-and-working-from-home-so-I'm-not-really-off days. Data from LinkedIn found that workers took an average of just 2.5 sick days in 2018. And the World Economic Forum reports that "presenteeism," or showing up at work despite being unwell, is on the rise.

Even when we do take time off, technology has a way of pulling us back in. According to a study from the US Travel Association, only 37 percent of senior executives say they fully disconnect from work while on vacation, even though 95 percent said they're aware of the benefits of unplugging. In other words, there is a major gulf between what we *know* we should be doing and what we actually do. With our smartphones keeping us connected to the work we've ostensibly left behind, it's no wonder that 58 percent of workers feel absolutely no reduction in stress from their vacations, and 28 percent return even more stressed than they were before they left, according to a study by Fierce, Inc., a company that provides leadership development and training.

HOW I THRIVE

MARK CUBAN, Dallas Mavericks owner and *Shark Tank* star

Put your phone in the gym locker before your workout.

This way, you won't be tempted by emails, group texts, or calls and can get a healthy dose of disconnection while you exercise. "If I work out or play basketball, I won't have my phone on me. And I don't feel like 'Oh my goodness, I have to go check my phone every few minutes.'"

THE TRUTH ABOUT TECH CREEP

While technology has made it harder than ever for us to set boundaries with our jobs and to create the time and space we need to recharge, our hyperconnectivity isn't just a work issue. We've given technology the front seat—the guest-of-honor status, really—in every aspect of our lives. Our phones follow us into the kitchen, the bedroom, the bathroom; they tag along during our commutes and doctors' appointments. They're the third wheel on dates, the intruding party-crasher during family time and all our social interactions.

Simply put, when we don't set boundaries with technology, we pay a price. Take sleep: our phones are repositories of everything we need to put away to allow us to sleep—our to-do lists, our inboxes, our anxieties. Plus, the blue light they emit suppresses melatonin, the hormone connected to sleep regulation. When it comes to mental health, there's plenty of research suggesting a link between heavy social media use and depression, especially in young people.

And being tethered to our devices can negatively affect our relationships and ability to connect with others. For example, a Pew study found that 89 percent of phone owners said they'd used their phones in their last social gathering, and 82 percent felt that when they do this it damages the interaction. It's gotten so bad that the phone doesn't even need to be turned on for it to negatively affect our relationships. Another study found that when two people are in a conversation, the mere presence of a phone can have, as the authors write, "negative effects on closeness, connection, and conversation quality." The mere presence of mobile phones can create a psychological hindrance.

Until 2019, when she joined Instagram, the award-winning actress and producer Jennifer Aniston was one of the last remaining social media holdouts in Hollywood. On the Thrive Global podcast, she spoke about her decision to abstain and mused about a time when our lives didn't revolve around our phones. "If *Friends* was created today, you would have a coffee shop full of people that were just staring into iPhones," she said. Our brains are wired to respond to stimuli, and few things are more stimulating than the pings and buzzes from our devices.

Research shows that people check their device every six and a half minutes—about 150 times a day. Even when we recognize that scrolling through social media is stressing us out, we cope with that stress by switching to another section of the same platform or app instead of just backing away from our phones, according to a study of Facebook users published in *Information Systems Journal*.

The ever-increasing creep of technology into our every waking moment makes it more challenging for us to renew and replenish ourselves, and it can just as easily strain our relationships. A lexicon has even emerged, pointing to how big the problem is. "Phubbing," for instance, refers to snubbing a partner in favor of your phone. In one Baylor University study that asked 175 men and women questions about their partners' smartphone use, 46 percent of respondents reported being phubbed by their partner. Phubbing has been linked with higher levels of relationship conflict. In a study published in the journal *Psychology of Popular Media Culture*, nearly three-quarters of women in committed relationships said that smartphones were negatively impacting their relationship and 62 percent said they contributed to spending less time with their partner.

HOW BURNOUT TAKES HOLD

Judging by our behavior, our relationship with our devices is the most important relationship we have. We're all exquisitely aware of the recharging routine of our phones, how often we need to do it, how long it takes, how long we can go without recharging it, where the nearest outlet is. We set up recharging shrines in every room in our homes, as well as in our cars and offices. If only we were this acutely attuned to our own recharging needs!

When our bodies send us signals that we're exhausted, stressed, or depleted—whether mentally, emotionally, or spiritually—instead of taking a break from technology or work to recharge our batteries, we push through. The effects of hitting Snooze on these warning signals can be seen in the prevalence of burnout—a phenomenon that's existed for ages but that the World Health Organization (WHO) officially acknowledged in 2019 by adding it to its International Classification of Diseases. According to WHO, burnout stems directly from "chronic workplace stress that has not been successfully managed." And it isn't an uncommon problem: a 2018 Gallup study of nearly 7,500 full-time employees found that 23 percent of employees reported feeling burned out very often or always.

> **HOW I THRIVE**
>
> **SUZY BATIZ**, founder of Poo~Pourri and Supernatural
>
> **Set an automatic Wi-Fi cut-off time every night.**
>
> "The Wi-Fi in my house is on a timer; it turns off at 9:30 every night and stays off until 6 a.m. I don't want the Wi-Fi signals disturbing my sleep. Houseguests don't always love it."

Despite burnout's very real costs, many of us don't take steps to address it. There's a collective delusion that burnout is simply the price we must pay for success. In a *New York Times* op-ed, "You Are Doing Something Important When You Aren't Doing Anything," Bonnie Tsui captured this well. Taking time for rest and renewal "can make us feel out of step with what the prevailing culture tells us," she wrote. "The 24/7 hamster wheel of work, the constant accessibility and the impatient press of social media all hasten the anxiety over someone else's judgment. If you aren't visibly producing, you aren't worthy."

According to the logic of hustle culture, any time spent not working or being plugged in is simply time wasted. But in reality, the burnout symptoms identified by the WHO—depletion and exhaustion, negativity and cynicism, reduced professional efficacy—are surefire recipes for failure, not success. In *Rest: Why You Get More Done When You Work Less*, Alex Soojung-Kim Pang shows us that the secret behind the breakthroughs by many of history's most creative authors, scientists, thinkers, and politicians is that they were very serious and disciplined about taking time to rest. That's because people perform better—and can stay in the game longer—when the work process includes time for unplugging and recharging.

RECHARGING OURSELVES

A popular way to respond to impending burnout is to take a vacation. But here's the thing: The restorative effects we tap into during vacations are fleeting if we go right back to the behaviors that were burning us out in the first place—if we don't *also* change the way we fundamentally work and live every day. After all, as with most other healthy habits—even basic ones like brushing our teeth—a short period of diligence can't make up for months and months of self-neglect. What we need is a commitment to recharging our internal batteries on a daily basis, because being proactive about preventing burnout in the first place is much better than trying unsuccessfully to make up for it.

At Thrive, one way we do this is through what we call Thrive Time. This practice is based on the recognition that, of course, getting results and meeting deadlines often require putting in extra time and going the extra mile. Thrive Time means taking time off to recover and recharge immediately after you've met the deadline, shipped the product, or worked over the weekend. It could be a few hours, a morning, a whole day, or even more. Taking Thrive Time isn't a reward, it's a responsibility. That's why it also often comes at the suggestion of a manager, part of whose job is maintaining team performance and being vigilant in guarding against burnout. Thrive Time, or intentional recovery, is about renewing what was depleted and giving yourself the resources to show up for what's next.

Importantly, Thrive Time does not count as vacation, or sick time, or other paid time off. The point is that recovery isn't separate from work; it's an essential part of work. Bonnie Tsui has another name for this kind of integrated recovery: fallow time. "I'm not talking about vacation or weekends," she wrote. "I'm talking about a more regular practice, built into our understanding of what work is. Fallow time is part of the work cycle, not outside of it."

It doesn't require a plane ticket or a full-on detox from technology. In fact, while digital detoxes—just like vacations—may seem like a good solution, they may prove only as effective as a diet detox. The downside—whether you're sipping kale smoothies or locking away your phone for a week—is that when the detox is over, it's easy to fall back into old, addictive habits. "If it takes unplugging to learn how better to live plugged in, so be it. But let's not mistake such experiments in asceticism for a sustainable way of life," writes Casey Cep in the *New Yorker*, in a piece called "The Pointlessness of Unplugging." "For most of us, the modern world is full of gadgets and electronics, and we'd do better to reflect on how we can live there than to pretend we can live elsewhere."

A more realistic and sustainable way to manage our relationship with technology and work is to use Microsteps. None of them require swearing off email or throwing away your phone. It's about setting boundaries. Dr. Fotini Markopoulou, the cofounder and CEO at doppel, a company that makes products focused on the relationship between our physical and our emotional state, admits that "going offline is a struggle—I am as addicted to my phone as everyone else, but I do what it takes to put it away. Currently I lock it away in a box every evening! It goes in its box at 9 p.m. and doesn't come out until 7 a.m."

That's an extreme approach, of course. And learning to set boundaries with your devices may become easier when you understand *why* you feel so attached to them. In his book,

Indistractable: How to Control Your Attention and Choose Your Life, behavioral designer Nir Eyal argues that understanding the internal triggers that lead to a gravitational pull of our devices is essential for creating a sustainable new relationship with technology. That means spending some time with your feelings to understand *why* you compulsively check your email after hours to see if your boss messaged you, scan Instagram even when you're enjoying the company of others, or open up Slack on your phone before you've even gotten off the elevator when leaving work. Cep's *New Yorker* piece put forth one theory that explains the "why": "What sex was for the Puritans, technology has become for us. We've focused our collective anxiety on digital excess."

Anxiety—or maybe even a lack of sex—is one explanation. But frustration, boredom, loneliness, sadness, and any other number of uncomfortable feelings can also act as triggers. In her book *Maybe You Should Talk to Someone*, the psychotherapist Lori Gottlieb, PhD, observed that "across the country—at coffee with friends, in meetings at work, during lunch at school, in front of the cashier at Target, and at the family dinner

---

HOW I THRIVE

MIKE POSNER, Grammy-nominated singer-songwriter

Each morning, put your phone on airplane mode until you've completed one goal that matters to you.

"I like to use my old phone which isn't connected to the internet as my alarm clock. Though I sometimes cave in, I prefer to not take my phone off of airplane mode until I've meditated, exercised, and launched into my goals for the day."

● ● ●

---

table—people were texting and tweeting and shopping, sometimes pretending to make eye contact and sometimes not even bothering." Gottlieb wondered: "Was it that people couldn't tolerate being alone or that they couldn't tolerate being with other people?" (Spoiler alert: probably both.)

The good news? While we might need help changing our behavior, we are no longer in a zombie state, using our phones without even a hunch that they're leaving us unfulfilled. We are discovering that while technology might be great at delivering what we want in the moment—including an escape from whatever discomfort we're trying not to feel—it's less great at giving us what we need over the long term. Technology promised us connection, along with endless efficiency, and hyperproductivity. But we're finally starting to understand that the results aren't always as promised. Very often, they are the opposite of what we are really seeking.

THE UPSIDE OF DOWNTIME

As more and more people recognize the importance of setting boundaries in our relationship with our devices in order to protect our humanity and well-being, experts are optimistic that we're entering a new era. BJ Fogg, a behavioral science researcher at Stanford University, has even predicted a shift toward a postdigital era, in which "being chained to your mobile phone" is stigmatized, not celebrated.

Of course, it's up to each individual to define what postdigital means for them. The phone stacking game is one ingenious solution that some, like NBA champion Andre Iguodala, rely on to practice unplugging. When friends meet for dinner, they put their phones in a stack in the middle of the table and the first one who checks their device before the bill comes has to pick up the check. The device-free dinners have led to better conversation and connection, Iguodala told Thrive. "It's a ritual . . . that's really good for us."

And what about Fogg's prediction that being glued to our phones will actually be seen as a negative? It's an attitude shift that might not be in our immediate future. But consider another transformation in public perception: how our views around smoking changed. In past eras, people believed wildly inaccurate things about cigarettes—they even watched with credulity as doctors went on television to recommend their favorite brands. The shift we saw culturally regarding smoking is proof that we can, in time, also break free from the collective delusion that our relationship with our devices is harmless.

Science is clearly showing us the impact of overwork and hyperconnectivity on our minds, bodies, and spirits—and we don't have to wait for a surgeon general's warning to start taking care of our well-being by unplugging and recharging. When it comes to machines, nonstop uptime is a good thing. But for human beings, there is a distinct upside to downtime: We need it to thrive. And we don't need to go to extremes to get it. We can adopt Microsteps that help us take charge of our technology, not the other way around.

• • • •

MICROSTEP DIARY

Lisa Chin Mollica, principal product designer

MICROSTEP: Each night, turn on Night Shift to make your phone's display easier on your eyes.

Why I Chose It

I always wanted to do this but was too lazy to look into how to set it up. It felt like something that I could set and forget, but that could potentially impact how I feel day to day. I hoped that practicing this Microstep would help me feel more calm at night.

What Happened

I have watched fellow engineers turn their devices on to Night Shift for years but never felt compelled to do so myself. The first night I did use it, I realized that turning my phone on at night no longer burned my eyes. The same would happen in the morning. It was just so soothing. I liked it so much that I turned the Night Shift on for my Mac desktop as well.

MICROSTEPS

When you wake up, don't start your day by looking at your phone. Instead, take at least one minute to breathe deeply or set your intentions for the day.

Turn off all notifications, except from those who need to reach you. The more our phone buzzes at us, the more it conditions us to release cortisol, which is the stress hormone.

Schedule time on your calendar for something that matters to you—outside of work. Whether it's going to the gym, going to an art gallery, or seeing friends, setting a reminder will help you hold yourself accountable.

Put away your phone and look up while commuting or running errands. Unplugging while on the move will help you connect with people, sights, and scenes around you—and take stock of what you're grateful for.

Don't look at your phone during mealtimes. If you're with friends, try playing the phone stacking game. Put your phones in the middle of the table. Whoever looks first picks up the check!

Put your phone away each time you socialize with friends or family. Whether it's dinner at home with your kids or out with friends, putting your device down allows you to be fully present in the moment and meaningfully connect with others.

Set aside just a couple of minutes each night to write in a journal. Writing by hand is a calming counterpoint to typing on devices, and it's a great way to collect your thoughts without digital distractions.

Delete one social media app from your phone. Using the clunkier browser version of an app—and having to enter your password each time—can create a pause long enough for you to consider what you'll really get out of scrolling through your feed.

When you take PTO (paid time off), shut off your email, calendar, and chat notifications. Unplugging from work in our off-hours helps us feel less stressed and more engaged when we're back.

As you brew your morning coffee or tea, focus on your breathing. Instead of watching TV or looking at your phone, focusing on your breathing helps you center yourself for the day ahead.

Each day, plan a small, fun activity to do after work. It can be easy to keep working until you go to sleep, but having something to look forward to after work can help you recharge. If you live with your family or roommates, it can become a nightly event to look forward to throughout the day.

Each night, turn on night mode to make your phone's display easier on your eyes. This adjustment will limit blue light from your phone screen and help you wind down for an easier transition to sleep.

HOW YOU CAN THRIVE

What are some ways your relationship with technology negatively impacts your well-being, productivity, and ability to connect with others?

What are some of your limiting beliefs about your screens and devices? For example, *I have to be "always on"* or *I'll miss something important.*

Did any of the science or stories you read in this chapter help you think about your challenges with technology in a new way?

What's one Microstep from this chapter that resonates with you that you could try today?

3

●●●●

NUTRITION AND HYDRATION

*O*ur nutrition choices are about much more than what we eat. *They're connected to our environment, our habits, and the mindset we bring to each day. If we're perpetually stressed and believe a life of ambition and achievement—or even just getting through our days—simply doesn't leave room for healthy food choices, we're probably not going to make nourishing ourselves a priority.*

But however busy we are, we can find moments throughout the day to recharge and connect—with others and ourselves—through our food choices. When we do, we not only set ourselves up for better physical and mental health, we can rediscover one of our biggest joy triggers. Maybe it's because I was raised by a mother who believed if you didn't eat something every twenty minutes something truly terrible would happen to you, but I try to be very intentional about finding time each day to connect with others over a meal, a quick bite, or a cup of coffee (as long as it's not too late in the day).

My personal favorite nutrition Microstep is the swap: find a go-to snack you love but that is not hyperprocessed or full of sugar—like pistachios or berries or almond butter. Or, if you are eating straight out of the bag, consider this story about an employee at a company we are working with who was addicted to Doritos. Her healthy eating

Microstep was to leave one more Dorito in the bag every day—one on the first day, two on the second day, and so on, until finally she was just licking the flavor off the Dorito! Eventually, she lost over one hundred pounds—an incredible demonstration of how taking small steps can have a big impact.

—Arianna Huffington

• ● ●

IF YOU HAD to put it simply, what does it mean to eat well? In the words of bestselling author and food expert Michael Pollan: "Don't eat anything your great-grandmother wouldn't recognize as food."

That's sage advice. But it's the tip of the iceberg.

From a behavioral perspective, the food choices we make aren't random. They're connected to our beliefs. And on the surface, these beliefs might not even be about food.

For example, if we believe recharging throughout the workday is a waste of time and productivity, then that belief impacts our eating habits. We're not going to value stepping away from our desk to have a healthy lunch and actually connect with our coworkers.

Beliefs like this are part of our burnout culture. We tell ourselves it's better to power through. We hear stories about entrepreneurs who built their companies while subsisting on a diet of unhealthy food and believe that we have to choose between taking care of ourselves and striving for success.

When we understand how our beliefs and our environment affect our eating choices, we empower ourselves to make better choices that can fuel our bodies, our minds, and our overall well-being.

THE BURNOUT DIET

When it comes to healthy eating, most of us know what we need to do—but we simply don't do it. We may make New Year's resolutions to cut back on sweets, or alcohol, or caffeine. When eating out, we may force ourselves to go with the salad instead of the fries. We may even experiment with fad diets that promise extraordinary transformations in a short time.

But what we often overlook—and the reason those quick-fix approaches frequently fail—is how our food choices are shaped by our beliefs. And the fact is, many of us believe that healthy food choices must be sacrificed in the name of achieving our goals and getting ahead.

"Our fast-paced, high-stress lives—and a work culture that too often celebrates burnout—can leave us feeling that suboptimal food choices are simply the price we pay for being successful," explains Maya Adam, a professor and director of the Stanford Center for Health Education Outreach at Stanford Medicine. When we buy into this belief, eating well becomes deprioritized—in fact, it might even seem like a nuisance or a waste of time. After all, who has the time or the headspace to plan a healthy meal when we're up against pressing work deadlines, full email inboxes that follow us home at night, and to-do lists that just seem to keep growing?

Along with sleep, nutrition is often written off as something that can—and must—be sacrificed on the way to success. Many entrepreneurs even boast about the unhealthy diets that fuel their start-ups.

"We're easily blinded by the headlines and possibilities of 'being our own boss,'" writes Arushi Mehta in *YSF Magazine*, which covers start-ups and entrepreneurship culture. "The problem is this: with all of the possibilities of success ahead, we often leave our health far behind. Many young entrepreneurs are, simply put, unhealthy."

Kari Sulenes, who directs a program to help support founders' well-being and reduce burnout, put it this way: "Expectations for health are so low that even when they have something like Lyme disease, they think that's just something to push through."

For Kara Goldin, success as a tech industry executive was fueled by Diet Coke—ten cans a day, to be exact. Drinking water felt boring to her, but her diet soda habit was contributing to serious health concerns, including weight gain, acne, and exhaustion. After a time, she left her tech job and founded Hint, Inc., a company specializing in bottled water flavored with natural fruit and no added sugar or sweetener. Part of her mission is to raise awareness about health issues including obesity and type 2 diabetes. "I'm

---

HOW I THRIVE

MICHELLE OBAMA, former first lady

Add a vegetable or fruit to every meal.

"Choosing a healthy diet isn't about deprivation, it's about balance. It's about moderation. Like I tell my kids, as long as you eat fruits and vegetables at every meal, you'll be okay if you have pizza or ice cream every once in a while. The problem is when the treats become the habits."

● ● ●

---

trying to spread the word that as a society we're in trouble," she told the BBC. "I really believe that we can help consumers get their health back in all parts of the world."

For Marissa Badgley, founder of Reloveution, a consultancy company striving to create more sustainable workplaces, the demands of being a founder led her to sacrifice key elements of her own health. While she felt driven to work long hours on projects she cared deeply about, her commitment came with a cost. As she told *Business Insider*, "I wasn't eating well, drinking enough water, exercising more than the walk to the printer, or spending any real quality time with friends or family, all things that I consider essential to keeping myself going." It wasn't until an ER visit for chest pains that she realized the need to prioritize her own well-being.

Even the former first family got caught in a wave of eating for convenience while rushing from one work and family commitment to another. "I began to see the pattern we were in. With Barack gone all the time, convenience had become the single most important factor in my choices at home," Michelle Obama wrote in *Becoming*. "We'd been eating out more. With

> ### HOW I THRIVE
>
> **MARIA MENOUNOS**, TV personality and entrepreneur
>
> ## Take a few minutes to think about one small way you can improve your eating this week.
>
> "I'm on a journey to keep getting better, and so I'm constantly seeking new information, and new ways to improve. I think eating well is really important to thriving, so I really try hard to feed my body good, positive fuel."

less time to cook, I often picked up takeout on my way home from work. In the mornings, I packed the girls' lunch boxes with Lunchables and Capri Suns. Weekends usually meant a trip to the McDonald's drive-through window after ballet and before soccer. None of this, our doctor said, was out of the ordinary, or even all that terrible in isolation. Too much of it, though, was a real problem."

When we strive so relentlessly and breathlessly after success as the world defines it, it becomes all too easy to decide that healthy eating isn't all that important. But the science shows that poor food choices profoundly—and negatively—affect the very things that help us succeed: our mental and physical health, our concentration, our productivity, and our decision-making. When we make room for healthy eating choices, we see benefits in all parts of our lives, including work. We also experience a lot more satisfaction knowing we're making choices that serve us instead of sabotage us.

MORE THAN JUST FUEL

Poor eating isn't like some other bad habits where the effects take years to manifest. Our eating and drinking choices can provide nearly instantaneous changes—for better and for worse—in our mood, energy, and performance. One Brigham Young University study of nearly 20,000 American workers, for instance, reported that an unhealthy diet is associated with as much as a 66 percent increased risk of productivity loss.

But we don't need external research for proof of how an unhealthy diet can derail us. We just need to look at our own internal data. Think of the sluggish slump we experience after wolfing down a sad desk lunch made up of whatever can be cobbled together from the office kitchen. Or the impossibility of concentrating after loading up on sugary foods because nothing else was available. Or the sleepless nights that can result from leaning on caffeine to power us through a busy day.

Ah, caffeine! As a culture, we prize it for its power to (temporarily) make us more alert and boost our energy. And for many people, every cup of coffee feels like a joy trigger. "Don't talk to me until I've had my coffee" is practically our national mantra, muttered daily by overtired people across the country. When overwork takes hold and we don't get enough shut-eye to feel refreshed and awake, we resort to a steady caffeine drip throughout the day.

But our overdependence on caffeine is both a cause and effect of burnout. Just think about the way so many of us drink our coffee—on the run, amping ourselves up with caffeine rather than actually recharging ourselves, just to speed up even more. Speed is not what we're seeking at midnight when we're desperately trying to sleep, but that's what we inevitably get. Caffeine has a half-life

> ### HOW I THRIVE
>
> **BIANCA BOSKER**, journalist and *New York Times* bestselling author
>
> **Instead of rushing out the door with your coffee in hand, take a few minutes to sit down and mindfully savor what's in your cup.**
>
> "[The first thing I do when I get out of bed is] make a pot of tea. It buys me time to clear my head before I really have to start thinking for the day. I also enjoy smelling the tea leaves—it's a little jolt of stimulation that gets me going."

of five to six hours, which means it takes about twenty-four hours for a cup of coffee to work its way out of our system. It's a ride we can't get off: we're tired during the day and wired during the night.

With caffeine and eating in general, that power-through mentality actually weakens our ability to perform at our best. So if you've been using the "food is just fuel" analogy to justify a poor diet, it's time to get a new motto. "This analogy is misleading," writes Ron Friedman, a psychologist and expert on the science of workplace excellence, in the *Harvard Business Review*.

"With fuel, you can reliably expect the same performance from your car no matter what brand of unleaded you put in your tank. Food is different. Imagine a world where filling up at Mobil meant avoiding all traffic and using BP meant driving no faster than 20 miles an hour. Would you then be so cavalier about where you purchased your gas?"

HOW I THRIVE

ASHLEY WILKING, fitness influencer

Look for little ways to set up your environment to make staying hydrated easier.

"I keep a liter of water beside my bed. It's easy to forget to hydrate during the busy day, so I try to down the entire thing before I leave the apartment."

THE MENTAL HEALTH CONNECTION

We tend to think of nutrition in physical terms. And of course, our food choices impact our bodies and our physical health.

But small changes to our eating habits can also yield significant improvements to our mental health.

"Americans routinely change what they eat in order to lose weight, control their blood sugar levels, and lower artery-clogging cholesterol," writes Richard Schiffman in the *New York Times*, citing the research of Dr. Drew Ramsey, a Columbia University expert on food and mental health. "But it is still rare for people to pay attention to the food needs of the most complex and energy-consuming organ in the body, the human brain."

So while we may be hyperwary of putting on a few extra pounds, we should also be aware of how our food choices affect other, less visible indicators of our well-being—for example, our mood, our ability to focus, and our ability to connect with others. Poor eating habits have been linked to common mental disorders including depression and anxiety. Nutrition has also been found to be an effective part of a treatment plan for mental disorders once they start. In a 2017 study out of Australia's Deakin University, researchers looked at whether dietary changes could help people with depression. Half the people in the study were given nutritional counseling to change their eating (with a

---

HOW I THRIVE

DAMBISA MOYO, global economist and author

If you're not crazy about the taste of plain water, look for add-ins that make it more enjoyable to encourage you to drink more.

"Have a cup of hot water, lemon, and ginger." Bonus: ginger has anti-inflammatory properties so you get an extra health boost in addition to the hydration.

focus on increasing the consumption of vegetables, fruits, whole grains, legumes, fish, lean red meats, olive oil, and nuts, while reducing their consumption of sweets, refined cereals, fried food, fast food, processed meats, and sugary drinks). The other half of study participants were given one-on-one social support. After twelve weeks, the people who made improvements to their diet showed significantly happier moods than those who didn't.

Another study found that people who increased their servings of fruits and vegetables over a two-year period reported more life satisfaction than those who didn't. And remarkably, the mood boost they experienced was equivalent to what an unemployed person feels after finding a job.

DRINK TO YOUR HEALTH

Water is the most important fuel we can give to our bodies. When we don't get enough, we become dehydrated. We may experience fogginess, fatigue, and find it hard to focus.

In other words, we certainly can't perform at our best. Our brains are made up of 75 percent water, and even mild dehydration can rob us of our full brain power. Studies by the University of Connecticut's Human Performance Laboratory, for example, showed that dehydration can adversely affect concentration, mood, and reasoning, and can also cause headaches and anxiety. Not exactly a recipe for a thriving life. On the flip side, when measured in response time, scientists found that staying hydrated can lead to an increase in productivity by as much as 14 percent.

···

Asking Yourself These Two Questions
Will Transform Your Approach to Eating

By Maya Adam, MD, director of Stanford Center
Health Education Outreach, Stanford Medicine

From the day we're born we enter a lifelong relationship with food.

And yet, most of us don't treat this relationship with the same respect and thoughtfulness as our human relationships: who we choose to date, or marry, or spend time with on any given evening.

Think about the questions you ask yourself when you're considering entering into a relationship with somebody. You probably ask:

1. Is this person good enough for me? And:
2. How much do I know about this person?

Your answers to these questions help you determine whether or not you choose to become involved. And no one would fault you for asking them before entering into something serious.

What if we thought about the act of eating—of putting food inside our bodies—as an equally intimate and important decision?

When we apply these same questions to our food decisions, we can improve our physical and mental health, and open up new ways for us to connect with others and enjoy life. Knowing where your food came from, who prepared it, and what's inside is key.

For example, if your dinner came from a farmers market and your spouse cooked it in your kitchen, you're going to have a certain level of trust and confidence that eating it will support your overall health. Compare that kind of food with something you'd find in the processed food aisles of any major supermarket. Can you even pronounce the ingredients on a bag of Doritos? Where did they come from and does the company that made them have a vested interest in your long-term health?

Asking these questions is a way of taking ownership of our food choices and making sure the foods we eat are worthy of us.

Is this food good enough for me? (Is it worthy of me?)

Do I know enough about where this food came from? (Can I trust that this food will delight me both in the moment I'm eating it and by making me feel good about my choices when I wake up tomorrow and the day after that?)

When you start asking these questions, you initiate a mindset shift. Whatever your current relationship with food, you have an opportunity to improve it.

• • • •

There is no formal recommendation for a daily amount of water people need. Broad recommendations—like drinking eight glasses per day—aren't based on exact science, as our fluid needs depend on our activity level, health status, and more. Whatever our own individual ideal may be, we have an opportunity to improve our well-being and performance by being just a little more intentional about hydrating—starting with the moment we wake up. We actually wake up dehydrated—simply by breathing while we sleep, we experience fluid loss. One easy Microstep to put into practice each morning is to make a point to hydrate and replenish what was lost while sleeping—before checking your phone.

DIGESTING A MINDSET SHIFT

Ultimately, our relationship with food is not just what we eat and drink but the attitudes that we bring to the table (literally).

We have more power than we realize to build nutrition habits that fuel a life of peak well-being and performance. But before we can take action we need to get really honest about our beliefs.

And we need to remember that food can be a source of joy and connection in our fast-paced, always-on world. Instead of viewing mealtimes and breaks as obstacles to success, we can view them as oases in our day—little opportunities to be present with ourselves and others and bring a little more perspective to our lives. And if that little voice in your head tells you that actually sitting down to eat lunch at work or taking a walk and healthy snack break with a colleague is going to torpedo your productivity, don't listen to it. Instead, think of these activities as small investments in yourself, your relationships, and your success. According to research at the Center for Talent Innovation published in the *Harvard Business Review*, when people feel like they belong at work, they are more productive, motivated, and engaged—and 3.5 times more likely to reach their fullest potential.

As Maya Adam, the Stanford food expert, writes, "Food can be a partner that drags you down and depletes your physical and mental health—the kind of partner your friends and family wish you'd break up with. Or it can be a partner that is truly worthy of you, supporting you in your life's journey, building you up, and bringing you joy. The choice is yours."

Making this choice doesn't require overhauling your diet or saying goodbye to the foods you love. Far from it! With Microsteps, you can make small changes and build healthy eating habits that will have a big impact—not just on your physical health but on every aspect of your life.

MICROSTEP DIARY

Rebecca Lerner, creative project manager

MICROSTEP: Set a daily caffeine cutoff.

Why I Chose It

I often use caffeine (coffee specifically) as an afternoon social out-ing/way to make my afternoon more exciting. However, there's a definite trade-off—I don't sleep nearly as well on days when I have coffee at 4 or 5 p.m. I wanted to cut down to one cup of coffee per day in the morning.

What Happened

I did my Microstep every day—I found it pretty easy to simply switch out my cup of coffee with a cup of decaf tea, which made me feel like I wasn't fully giving up my afternoon beverage break.

My main learning from this challenge was that it's easier to make a swap than to simply cut a food or beverage out of your life. Also, I learned that having an accountability buddy is vital. Everyone in my life knew that I wasn't drinking caffeine after 2 p.m. so no one was tempting me to grab coffee with them. A support system is key!

MICROSTEPS

Swap a healthy treat for your go-to sugary comfort food. If you find yourself reaching for unhealthy comfort foods, find a delicious snack that still feels like an indulgence but without the processed sugar. Try a bowl of berries instead of a cinnamon bun, or a fruit smoothie instead of ice cream.

Swap one sugary beverage a day with water. Sugar is proven to increase inflammation in our bodies, which limits our immune response. If you want, add a slice of lemon to make the water more flavorful.

Read the label on a food item in your home you think is healthy. Many foods—including cereals, juices, jams, and even bread—are loaded with sugar, even though they're labeled as healthy. A glance at the label will quickly boost your awareness so you can buy a different brand or swap it for something truly healthy.

Sit down when you eat, even for a few minutes. Mindless eating can lead us to consume more calories and experience bloating. If you can, choose a place to eat that's not the same place you work. Make it a meal!

Drink a glass of water when you wake up in the morning. Before checking your phone, make a point to hydrate and replenish what was lost while you were sleeping.

Keep a reusable water bottle at your desk and fill it each time you get up to use the restroom. You'll avoid the temptation of soda and other sugary drinks. Plus, refilling your bottle throughout the day will provide you with much-needed breaks and opportunities to connect with others.

Schedule an afternoon water break. Do this instead of taking a snack break. Studies have shown that mild dehydration can present as hunger and can even lead to overeating.

At each meal, note the flavor, look, and texture of your food. Being mindful of the experience of eating can help you feel more satisfied by nutritious foods.

Restore your energy and maintain hydration through the day by eating water-rich foods. Celery, strawberries, oranges, and yogurt are a few examples of foods that can help with hydration.

Bring your lunch to work, even just once a week. Take control and be intentional about what you put in your body by packing your own lunch.

HOW YOU CAN THRIVE

What are some eating choices you make that leave you feeling unhealthy, depleted, or unfulfilled?

Now, take a step back. How might these choices be connected to your environment and daily habits—even habits that have nothing to do with food?

What are your limiting beliefs about food? For example, *I'm too busy to eat lunch* or *Powering through on caffeine and packaged food is what I have to do because I'm so busy.*

Did any of the science or stories in this chapter help you think about your challenges with nutrition or hydration in a new way?

What's one Microstep from this chapter that resonates with you?

4

• • • •

MOVEMENT

*T*here's nothing easier to place at the bottom of our to-do lists than exercise and movement. We'd love to, we tell ourselves, but there's just not enough time in the day. The problem with that is there are also few things more important to our well-being than getting up regularly and moving around.

It's not just our schedules that get in the way, it's also the fact that the physical world so many of us work in now doesn't make it easy to get physical activity. Sitting down all day and looking at screens isn't just bad for us, it's very bad for us. There's a reason why health experts have described being sedentary as the new smoking.

We often think of our physical and mental health as being somehow separate, but they're deeply interconnected. The benefits of physical activity are as good for our minds as they are for our bodies. Movement makes us more creative, allows us to disconnect, and recharges us. If you want more energy, simply expend some by moving.

Another obstacle that gets in the way of movement is the idea that it has to be exercise, and that you have to be an exercise person to do it. But when we think of exercise simply as movement, it becomes something that we can all do. Movement is about just that, *moving. It's critical for every aspect of our well-being. And all you need to start is to take a literal Microstep.*

One of my favorite movement Microsteps is the walking meeting. Many of my best ideas have come while walking or hiking with a friend. And I get some of my most focused reading done while I'm on the stationary bike. At the Thrive offices, we all have standing desks. I love looking around and seeing the constantly changing configuration of Thrivers going up and down.

One of my favorite phrases is solvitur ambulando*: "It is solved by walking." It refers to the fourth-century-BC Greek philosopher Diogenes's response to the question of whether motion is real. To answer, he got up and walked. As it turns out, there are many problems for which walking is the solution. In our culture of overwork, burnout, and exhaustion, how do we tap into our creativity, our wisdom, our capacity for wonder?* Solvitur ambulando.

—Arianna Huffington

● ● ●

THERE'S NO DOUBT that exercise is good for us. Hailed as a "miracle drug" by the Academy of Medical Royal Colleges and "one of the best things people can do to improve their health" by the Centers for Disease Control and Prevention, physical activity is one of the keys to a thriving life. Exercise is scientifically linked to lowered stress levels, improved brain function, and even decreased risk of Alzheimer's disease later in life. And the benefits of physical activity go beyond the physical self. It has the power to transform our mood and even spark our next eureka moment.

Yet for all that physical activity does for us, finding time for it can be challenging—and even more difficult to keep up with as a lifelong habit. It's a problem on a global scale: one in four people worldwide are physically inactive, according to the World Health Organization. We know how important it is to get moving, be active, and get the blood pumping, but somehow it never rises to the level of a priority, especially when more sedentary activities—often involving screens—are crying out for our attention at every hour of the day and night.

In this chapter, we expand our definition of movement and exercise, and we explore the mindsets that limit our ability to live an active, thriving life. We also share small, creative ideas for bringing more movement into our lives every day that don't require a major life overhaul. With Microsteps, we'll see that building healthier habits is entirely possible, and that we can spot opportunities for movement in our days where we might have not seen them before.

THINKING OUTSIDE THE GYM

Part of the problem is this: Our definition of exercise needs a refresh. When we hear the word *exercise*, we think of schlepping to the gym, running a 5K, or lifting heavy weights. These are all perfectly healthy and valid pursuits, but for many of us, for various reasons, they're just never going to happen. A narrow definition of exercise only makes it easier to avoid.

But just as with sleep, nutrition, and other building blocks of our well-being, we pay a price when we skimp on physical activity. And when we *do* make a point to exercise, the benefits

TRAINING FOR AN IRONMAN TRIATHLON
MADE ME A BETTER ENTREPRENEUR

Starting a business requires a leap of faith. . . . It takes confidence to turn down a high-paying and more stable corporate career to follow your entrepreneurial pursuits. And you need confidence to put your reputation, financial capital, and physical and emotional well-being on the line.

Similarly, triathletes must develop self-confidence. You will run into challenges and have to face your worst fears, whether you're a pro or a beginner. Overcoming those doubts starts with silencing your inner critic, and learning to reframe your negative self-talk. . . .

I've found that the confidence I've developed from launching a business fuels my ability in endurance sports, and vice versa. When I'm faced with a challenging business situation, I recall how I taught myself to swim, bike, and run and, with the help of some amazing friends, coaches, and loved ones, completed an Ironman triathlon. I tell myself that if I could do that, then I can do anything.

—Ryan Frankel, founder of This App Saves Lives

go well beyond any generic idea of getting in shape. One study found that people who engaged in aerobic exercise at least five days a week were 43 percent less likely to report upper respiratory symptoms than their less-active counterparts. Another study, published in 2017 in the *British Medical Journal*, found that people who regularly biked to work decreased their risk of cancer and heart disease by 45 percent and 46 percent, respectively. Moreover, research shows that making your commute more active could also help you avoid getting sick.

A broad world of movement and exercise is at our disposal. There are plenty of ways that we can get creative with physical activity, and sneak some extra steps into our routines without going to the gym. And these small strategies make a difference. William Kraus, a professor at Duke University and the author of a 2018 study that links small bursts of exercise to longevity, told the *New York Times*, "The little things that people do every day can and do add up and affect the risk for disease and death." For example, if you take public transportation to work, you can get off one stop earlier to walk the rest of the way (added bonus: our brains release neurotransmitters while we walk that help us make better decisions and focus). If you drive, you can park at the outer edge of the parking lot. It sounds like nothing, but science shows that all physical activity counts—even the micro stuff.

REFRAMING OUR RELATIONSHIP WITH TIME

Here's another hitch: How on earth are we supposed to make time for exercise when we're so *busy* all the time? How many times have you pledged to change your sedentary ways, only to excuse yourself because you "just don't have the time"? If you've been there—and we've all been there—don't judge yourself. But understand that when we have a scarcity mindset about our time (a condition only worsened by associating exercise with long slogs to the gym), we may be less likely to fill the time we do have in meaningful ways. By shifting our perspective, we'll be more able to see pockets in our day that are waiting to be filled with purposeful activity.

In fact, a 2019 study from the Centers for Disease Control and Prevention and the RAND Corporation revealed that most of us do have extra hours at our disposal. The researchers looked at Census Bureau data on how American adults spend their time on a typical day, setting aside time devoted to essential, nondiscretionary activities like sleeping, eating, grooming, working or going to school, cooking, and cleaning. What they found is that we have, on average, about three hundred minutes of discretionary time to use. That clocks out to more than five hours per day. And it turns out we devote very little of this time to movement and exercise: just fourteen minutes a day, on average, for women, and twenty-five minutes for men.

HOW I THRIVE

DARA TORRES, Olympic swimmer

Have your exercise gear set up the night before so your morning goes smoothly.

"Have everything set up the night before so my morning goes smoothly (i.e., my four dogs' breakfasts, my daughter's lunch, my clothes laid out, my daughter's school uniform laid out, etc.). . . . Makes my mornings much easier!"

So how can we make sure our free time doesn't simply fall by the wayside? We can take a Microstep, like booking time on our calendar to get moving. The Mayo Clinic recommends treating our workout time just as we would any other kind of appointment we wouldn't want to miss. This simple practice can make a big difference.

And remember: movement time doesn't need to be long to be effective. Recent science shows the value of even small bursts of physical activity. In 2018, the American Heart Association updated its guidelines on physical activity, correcting an earlier misconception that exercise needs to be a minimum of ten minutes to be effective. Instead, "the total amount is what matters," they write. If we only have five minutes available, we can spend one minute of that time doing jumping jacks, or dropping low and doing a plank. We can stretch at our desk (a highly beneficial movement we explore in greater detail later in this chapter). We can take a cue from Boris Kodjoe, the actor and cocreator of KOFIT, an exercise and nutrition app made specifically for busy families. Kodjoe doesn't even attempt to make his workouts longer than twenty minutes. By making his sweat sessions bite-sized, he knows he'll always have time for them.

STICKING WITH IT

Movement is a mental practice as much as it is a physical one. That's why so many professional athletes and fitness buffs say that the first step of training is about training our mindset. This is backed by research. A fascinating study published in *Health Psychology* suggests that our mindsets about our fitness affects how fit we actually are. Researchers from Stanford University

HOW PRIORITIZING MY WELL-BEING
BOOSTED MY SUCCESS AS A LEADER

Instead of letting my health slide during a particularly stressful time at work, I doubled down on it. I reasoned that if ever there was a time for healthy living, it is during times of greater stress and more work. In the past, I might have said that I felt so tired and miserable that I "deserved" to eat a bag of Goldfish crackers and drink more wine and skip working out. This time I pushed myself to think about "deserving" good, healthy foods and physical movement throughout my day, which were the things that *really* make me feel better.

I worked on adding more protein, especially fish, and vegetables to my diet, and I cut out some carbohydrates and sugar. I worked on finding times to get up and move throughout the days, and I scheduled workouts into my travel calendar. The hardest part may have been getting enough sleep. I am a morning person, and I get up early, but a number of my colleagues tend to work and stay up later. Thus, we had a lot of late-night email exchanges going around. I just had to remind myself that those would be there in the morning, and if anyone had an urgent reason to reach me, they could always do so. News flash: No calamity occurred because I went to bed at 10:00 p.m.!

—Deborah Platt Majoras,
chief legal officer at Procter & Gamble

found that, regardless of actual physical activity, respondents who identified as less active had a 71 percent higher increased risk of early death than participants who identified as more active. In addition to causal factors like the placebo effect and the fact that feeling less active than others can lead to stress and depression, the researchers say the findings illustrate a clear connection between our mindsets and our motivation.

Additional research reveals that our motivations for working out can actually predict how frequently we exercise. For example, people who were primarily motivated by intrinsic reasons—like enjoyment, challenging themselves, or stress management—worked out more frequently than those with extrinsic motivations, like getting the perfect body, or the social status that they think may come with being fit.

That's why it's important to move beyond a narrow definition of exercise that revolves mostly around losing weight or making our body look a certain way. There's nothing wrong with setting big, ambitious fitness goals, but we're far more likely to reach them when we shift our focus to Microsteps that are too small to fail.

In some exercise settings—like on a treadmill that tells us how many calories we're burning—it can be hard to look beyond the metrics. That's why Traci Copeland, a master trainer for Nike, recommends being mindful of tech while exercising. "I think technology can be a good way to measure your goals, your miles ran, and your calories burned, but beyond that it can disrupt a natural flow," she told Thrive. "When I'm in dance class, I'm not counting calories I've burned, I'm just enjoying my workout."

Copeland illustrates the power of connecting to your "why" when it comes to exercise. Posting impressive stats or moving closer to the body you want are fine rewards, but have you considered how exercise is an investment in yourself in other ways? Next time you lace up your running shoes or climb onto the stationary bike, take a moment to ask yourself why you're doing it: you might find that exercise improves your life in ways you hadn't considered.

For example, as Luke Milton, a former rugby player and trainer on E!'s *Revenge Body*, told Thrive, exercise can help us be as present as possible for the people who matter most. "Consistent exercise helps you to achieve a healthy lifestyle, and keeps you more energetic for your kids, husband or wife, or your mates."

As Milton suggests, it's okay if our motivations are extrinsic so long as they don't make us feel bad about ourselves. But in order to maximize the benefits of a workout and stick with our movement plan, it can be helpful to reframe our motivations. Before we hop on the bike, for example, we can pause to appreciate how exercise activates pleasure in our brains. Scientists say

---

HOW I THRIVE

BORIS KODJOE, actor and cocreator of KOFIT

Exercise for five minutes in the morning.

"Let's say I have five minutes. I would literally roll out of bed, use the bathroom, and then come back in my bedroom and I would jog in place for a minute to warm up, and then pick four very basic exercises for my entire body: squats, push-ups, sit-ups, and maybe some deadlift swan dives. I would do twenty seconds of each, and do that again two more times. That's five minutes."

● ● ●

that some forms of exercise, like running, can produce a natural high, due to the release of dopamine and endocannabinoids in our brains. So sure, exercising may bring us closer to having the body we've always wanted. But it also makes our heart stronger, lowers our risk of diabetes, and decreases stress levels. Using these scientifically proven health benefits as an additional motivation, we can take Microsteps toward a life where movement becomes a habit—and a source of meaning in our days.

Another way to help make movement a habit is to make it social. Celebrity fitness trainer Kira Stokes calls it "sweat unity," when you make a pact with a friend or family member to try a new exercise class or method together, or even when you simply check in on one another and track your goals. A study from 2018 that looks at data from 1.2 million people in the United States underscores the benefits of sweat unity. The cross-sectional analysis, published in the *Lancet Psychiatry*, found that people who exercised regularly reported one-and-a-half fewer poor mental health days than those who didn't exercise—and those who exercised on a *team* enjoyed the highest levels of mental well-being. This finding aligns with previous research showing the importance of having social support from peers, which provides encouragement and promotes community and connection.

INCORPORATING MORE
MOVEMENT INTO OUR DAY

The architecture of our modern lives makes so many things possible—a world of connectivity at our fingertips, for instance, and conveniences that would have been unimaginable a generation ago. But it doesn't leave much room for movement.

In fact, our relationship with technology is closely tied to a more sedentary lifestyle. Remember those three hundred minutes per day of discretionary time? We spend a huge number of them looking at our phones, leading to what's known as text neck. So much of our work, relationships, entertainment, and more leads us to spend long hours typing on computers, which can lead to carpal tunnel syndrome.

Our increasing reliance on technology only makes it more important to make exercise and movement a priority. One in four people spend more than eight hours a day sitting. Findings from a 2020 study, published in *JAMA Oncology*, suggest that extended sitting is linked with greater chances of dying from cancer later in life. In an interview with the *Los Angeles Times*, James Levine, a professor of medicine at the Mayo Clinic said, "Sitting is more dangerous than smoking, kills more people than HIV, and is more treacherous than parachuting."

There's hope, though. Studies show that even light movement throughout the day can help reduce the harmful effects of what some experts call the sitting disease. Even a simple stretch at your desk can have a profound effect. This kind of little interruption—what researchers from a 2016 study call microbursts of activity—can prompt an observable boost in energy and mood, countering fatigue and even reducing snack cravings. When we stretch, we're not only promoting circulation through parts of the body that may have been tight or knotted, we're also releasing our breath from its habitual stress patterns: shallow and stuck in our chest and throat. It's an easy way to boost well-being at work, whether that's in an office, at home, or somewhere else. When we give our body a break from work, our mind will follow suit.

Going a step beyond stretching, getting our heart rate up during the workday has been found to boost job performance. Walking, for example, can boost our creative output by an average of 60 percent (we explore this in more detail in the chapter about creativity). Walking has also been shown to break down barriers between managers and employees. At Thrive Global's New York office, we have a treadmill (with an attached desk if people want to walk slowly while answering emails!) and a SoulCycle bike, along with exercise balls and some weights for people to use on work breaks. And a group convenes regularly for stretch breaks. Ryan Holmes, the cofounder of Hootsuite, a digital platform that helps companies manage their social media accounts, says he couldn't have scaled the company to where it is today had he not incorporated fitness into the ethos of the brand. Before they could afford the gym that's in their office now, Holmes says they encouraged employees to bike to work, had yoga balls brought in that people could use as chairs, and "made it clear that anyone could block off an hour for exercise during the day," so long as it didn't interfere with deadlines.

HOW I THRIVE

HODA KOTB, co-anchor of the *TODAY* show and *TODAY with Hoda & Jenna*

Play a song you love while you exercise.

"If I'm stressed . . . I put on a country music playlist because nothing makes me happier than running in Central Park with country music blasting."

• • •

If you'd like to take exercise breaks during the day, but your workplace doesn't have an open rule or policy about it, try raising the issue, with some compassionate directness, to your manager. Too often, we assume we know the answer to something before we actually take steps to find out, allowing ourselves to feel disappointed or resentful of something that may not even be real. During your next 1:1 with your manager, or the next time you sit down to talk to each other if you don't have frequent check-ins, ask her if it would be okay for you to take a midday workout class, once a week. She may say no, but she may say yes—and then, not only will you be boosting your own health, but you'll be creating change at your workplace for you and for others. If this type of conversation feels out of reach, remember that there are other ways to get your heart rate up midday that don't involve a class or something formal. Take a short walk outside. Find a partner to stretch with during a break (you may quickly find there are others who want to join up). At your desk—or anywhere, really—reach both arms above your head and clasp your

---

HOW I THRIVE

NORA MINNO, certified personal trainer and star of the Daily Burn's "DB365"

Next time you make plans with friends, choose an activity that's movement-focused.

"I also try and plan meetings or meetups with people that don't just revolve around sitting and eating or drinking. I'll invite someone to meet me for a walk and talk, or to take a fitness class together instead of going out for cocktails. There are lots of creative ways to take your meetings and social meetups on the move."

● ● ● ●

hands together, with your palms facing the ceiling. Keeping your hands clasped, reach up as high as you can and hold for five seconds. If there are stairs in your building, take a few minutes to walk up and down a few flights. This is a particularly effective aerobic workout, as research shows that short, intense exercise can rapidly build and maintain fitness and health, even when the workout is extremely brief.

WALK THIS WAY

One of the most beneficial ways to move our bodies is so simple it's easy to miss. If you're looking for a healthy activity that doesn't require expensive equipment or long hours at the gym, walking might be the best place to start.

Walking is one of the most studied forms of exercise, and its benefits can be seen in nearly every aspect of our lives. A study of over forty thousand Canadians found that people who live in walkable neighborhoods have lower rates of cardiovascular disease. Walking in nature, specifically, can help reduce negative rumination, according to another study. And another study, this one by Dutch researchers, shows that those who live within one kilometer of a park or wooded area suffer lower rates of depression and anxiety than those who don't. Walking as a tool for dealing with depression is no small thing when you consider that, according to the World Health Organization, more than 350 million people worldwide suffer from it. But even if we don't live surrounded by trees and greenery, we can find ways to get in a short walk, with all the benefits it brings.

Many people believe that getting their 10,000 steps is the gold standard for walking each day, and fitness trackers often use this figure as a goal to promote optimal health. But the number, which originated decades ago from a Japanese marketing campaign for a pedometer, isn't actually grounded in science. I-Min Lee, a researcher at Brigham and Women's Hospital, set out to determine how many steps we *actually* need to maintain good health. Her research, which she said was "surprising," revealed that participants who took 4,000 steps in a day got a boost in longevity compared to those who didn't. What's more, the benefits actually maxed out at around 7,500 steps!

The benefits of getting up and walking—of moving—go beyond our bodies. A study led by University of Illinois researchers shows that walking three times a week for forty minutes at one's own natural pace helps combat the effects of aging and increases brain connectivity and cognitive performance. Even a few minutes here and there, whenever you have the time, will make a difference.

In Japanese culture, there's a concept called *Ma*, which can be loosely translated as the essential space, or interval or gap, between things, and the importance of creating and fully experiencing such spaces. So whether we are just taking a walk without wanting to get anywhere in particular, or whether we are walking toward a destination, walking to connect two places, the space, the interval in between, can be important. It can, in fact, be the point.

Finally, walking is a great habit-stacking activity. That is, you can create a healthy new habit by stacking it onto an existing habit. While you're walking, you might use this time to call a loved one, think of three things you're grateful for, or engage in a few minutes of conscious breathing.

· · · ·

MICROSTEP DIARY

Gregory Beyer, director of content strategy

MICROSTEP: Schedule time on your calendar for exercise.

Why I Chose It

Last year my doctor gave me some tips for simple workouts you can do anywhere—no gym membership, no big time commitment. This year I'm going to surprise him with the news that I've taken his advice. The best opportunity for exercise I have is right when I wake up, so I've committed to 50 push-ups and 50 jumping jacks in the morning. My hope was to make this ritual into something so automatic I don't even think about it.

What Happened

I probably average five out of seven days a week. I play basketball one night a week, and run pretty hard during those games. So some Tuesday mornings I'm sore and let myself off the hook. I do feel physically stronger, and my endurance is probably better, but the satisfaction is more mental. I said I was going to do something, and I did it. And I feel like I can build on my current ritual to make it more rigorous. Best of all, on many mornings I felt motivated to go beyond what I required of myself, sometimes doubling the routine.

There really is something important about the "micro" aspect of a Microstep. It's that smallness that helps you get past all the excuses you make for yourself. Every morning, I came up with all sorts of excuses not to do my Microstep. But since my workout took three minutes tops, there was never any legitimate excuse not to do it. My Microstep commitment was definitely successful, and I plan to keep going.

MICROSTEPS

Get off public transportation one stop earlier to walk the rest of the way. Our brains release neurotransmitters while we walk that help us make better decisions and focus.

Schedule time on your calendar for exercise. You wouldn't miss an important meeting or doctor's appointment, so blocking out movement time on your calendar in the same way can help you shift your mindset to prioritize your physical well-being. Research shows that even a few short and sweet minutes of movement in your day can make a positive impact.

Take a one-minute stretch break whenever you can throughout the day. Frequent movement fuels your body and mind. Stand up, change positions, stretch—anything to get your blood flowing.

Every time you exercise, take a minute to acknowledge that you showed up for yourself. Celebrating even small wins helps make habits stick.

Find one moment to sneak some extra steps into your daily routine. Even on a packed day you can find creative ways to move. Try taking the stairs instead of the elevator or park at the outer edge of a parking lot and walk to your destination.

Every time you brush your teeth, do a few squats. Stacking a new habit on top of an existing one is a great way to add movement with no extra time.

Build recovery time into your day. Take a tip from top athletes who introduce small recovery rituals into their game.

Simply stop what you're doing and bring your awareness to the palms of your hands or the soles of your feet, or both. Let your awareness stay there for a minute, and feel the tension leaving your body.

Once a day, take a short walk and focus on your breathing. You can still your mind even when you're moving your body. If you're in a place filled with noise and distractions, a quiet walk once or twice a day can help bring you into closer contact with yourself, your breath, and the world beyond your workplace.

Once a day, turn a sit-down meeting into a walking meeting. Walking side by side with a colleague, you'll be less likely to look at your devices, and the movement will get the creative juices flowing.

Whenever a call ends early, or when you get up to use the restroom, take an extra two minutes for a stretch break. You can use that time productively by reinvigorating yourself with movement.

HOW YOU CAN THRIVE

Even if we know the importance of exercise and moving our body, life tends to get in the way. What are some obstacles to moving more that you encounter on a regular basis?

What are some limiting beliefs you have about movement? For example, *I can't get exercise because I'm not a gym person* or *I'm too busy to make time for movement.*

Did any of the science or stories in this chapter help you think differently about how to fit movement into your day? How so?

What's one movement Microstep you read about that you can try putting into action right away?

5

FOCUS AND PRIORITIZATION

*T*he ability to focus is a valuable and increasingly rare commodity in our modern world.

And yet, so much of our workday is spent doing anything but focusing. A report by the McKinsey Global Institute found that only 39 percent of our day is spent doing task-specific work. The rest is email, tracking down information, tracking down colleagues, and all the other busywork black holes that suck up our time and consume our attention. Nor is the answer multitasking. As studies have shown, multitasking is a myth that mostly means doing a suboptimal job on two things at once.

Automation and AI and communication technology will continue to transform our workplace, and advances in these areas will, conversely, put a premium on the uniquely human ability to focus and do deep, creative, and sustained work. But to prepare for this inevitable future, we can look to the past. The philosophy of the Stoics is actually supremely practical. It helps us step outside of our thoughts and be aware of them instead of being imprisoned by them.

We can't live well unless we can work well—and we can't work well unless we live well. Being able to focus and get done what needs to get done is what allows us to declare an end to our day, unplug, and recharge for the next day.

And that starts by nurturing our ability to focus. It might seem impossible in a world in which we're being bombarded by "urgent" notifications, alerts, DMs, emails, texts, surprise calendar invites, and colleagues wondering, "Do you have a sec?" But we really can reclaim our attention. One of the Microsteps in this chapter is literally the first thing I do when I wake up each morning. Or, should I say, don't do. Instead of reaching for my phone the second my eyes open, I take a minute to breathe and set my intentions for the day. It may not sound like much, but that small moment of focus can stay with you all day.

—*Arianna Huffington*

• • • •

IT'S A NORMAL morning at work. You're on a conference call with your team—at the same time you're also answering "urgent" emails. You take a quick moment to respond to a text from your partner checking on dinner plans. You're also streaming news at low volume on the TV hanging on the wall and you have an eye on the stock market. A colleague pings you, looking for advice on a matter that needs to be handled—right now! You handle it—problem solved. A sip of coffee and you remember that you're still in a team meeting, and you quickly weigh in. Two more emails arrive and you reply to them before they can add to your inbox. Then a Slack notification informs you of a critical project update. And so it goes. . . .

If this kind of intensely frenetic scenario sounds famil- iar, you're not alone. Multitasking has become our de facto approach to work and life. Our ability to take on many tasks at once is often seen as positive, even commendable. And doing this is also unavoidable, largely because giving our full attention to anything—or anyone—is becoming more and more difficult in our hyperconnected world that has so many competing demands for our time and attention.

There's just one problem: Multitasking doesn't work. In this chapter, we dig into the myth of multitasking and explore how focusing and prioritizing well can lead to a more meaningful, productive, and rewarding way of working and living. We also hear from people from all walks of life who are harnessing the extraordinary power of focus.

We look not only at the science but also ancient wisdom about giving our attention to what really matters. The Stoics in particular, including Marcus Aurelius, Epictetus, and Seneca, remind us of how we tend to fill up our time with distractions, and instead how valuable it is to live in the moment.

> **HOW I THRIVE**
>
> **WANDA HOLLAND GREENE**, education expert
>
> **Color code your calendar to prioritize effectively.**
>
> "I color-code the entries in my Google calendar so that I can pay close attention to three things: self-care, family, and work."
>
> ● ● ●

MULTITASKING IS A MYTH

The widely held belief that we can multitask without sacrificing the quality of our attention is a fallacy. The brain simply can't fully focus when it's engaged in what's known as fragmented work. We often think we are being super-productive, checking things off, and maximizing productivity. But that's not what's really happening. A report published in the American Psychological Society's *Journal of Experimental Psychology* found that multitasking can cause productivity to drop as much as 40 percent.

This is even more true for those who think they're particularly good at multitasking. In one 2012 study, David Strayer, a professor of psychology at the University of Utah, found that the better people thought they were at multitasking, the more likely their performance was subpar. While Strayer identified a tiny minority of outliers he calls supertaskers, most of us pay a price when we try to focus on more than one thing at a time.

That's because interrupted work comes at a cost. As researchers from the University of California, Irvine, and the Institute of Psychology at Humboldt University in Berlin found, interruptions lead to "more stress, higher frustration, time pressure and effort." Earl Miller, a neuroscientist at MIT, puts it this way: "When we toggle

---

HOW I THRIVE

VALERIE WONG FOUNTAIN, managing director, Morgan Stanley

Write down a list of tasks and projects you want to complete.

"I quickly knock out anything that takes less than 5 minutes to do, whether by doing it myself or delegating it to someone else—it feels great to check off a completed task. Next, I prioritize the remaining items and put together a project plan for each. Finally, I roll up my sleeves and get to work—the sooner I tackle each, the sooner it is off my list."

● ● ●

THE SMALLEST BIT OF FRICTION

Like most people, my phone is probably the biggest distractor. The good news is I have two methods that have helped a lot.

The first is that, whenever possible, I leave my phone in another room (outside of my office) until lunch each day. This gives me at least three or four hours of uninterrupted time to work. What's remarkable is that I never really feel an urge to go get my phone even though I would certainly check it all the time if I had kept it with me. That's a strange thing about many habits: once the smallest bit of friction is added, they fade away.

The second is that I keep my phone permanently in Do Not Disturb mode when it is on me. This means my phone never beeps, buzzes, or chimes when I get a text or a call. You might think this backfires sometimes and I miss a call or something. However, the average adult checks their phone over 150 times per day and I'm no different. Even though my phone isn't buzzing, I'll check it every couple minutes when I have it on me. Odds are, I can call or text someone back within a few minutes. It hasn't been an issue yet.

—James Clear, author of *Atomic Habits: An Easy & Proven Way to Build New Habits & Break Bad Ones*

between tasks, the process often feels seamless, but in reality, it requires a series of small shifts." Each small shift results in a cognitive cost. For example, every time you switch between responding to emails and writing an important paper, you're draining precious brain resources and energy just to get back to where you started. Miller's advice is to avoid multitasking because "it ruins productivity, causes mistakes, and impedes creative thought. . . . As humans, we have a very limited capacity for simultaneous thought, we can only hold a little bit of information in the mind at any single moment."

The flow of interruptions and distractions can be relentless, but when you get out in front of it, you can take control of your time and give your attention to what is most important.

People were thinking about the value of attention long before email and iPhones came along. For the Stoics, it was about focusing on what we can control, including our attention and our reactions. There are so many things we all strive to get done, but to save time—and energy and attention—it pays to stop worrying about everything you can't change or do anything about. That includes many of those "urgent" questions or distractions draining our energy. It means being disciplined with your time. It means paying attention, which helps you to focus.

There are always going to be interruptions demanding our attention. In fact, 28 percent of the average workday is consumed by interruptions and the resulting recovery time. Those endless distractions drain our energy, and they can drain us to

---

HOW I THRIVE

HOWARD WEISS,
organizational psychologist

Break down a big goal into small daily steps.

"If I'm writing a book, I don't leave my goal as 'write this book.' If I do, I'm never going to write the book. A good friend of mine once told me a more effective strategy: 'A page a day is a book a year.'"

• • •

such an extent that it can be difficult for us to give our undivided attention to anything at all.

In Chapter 2 and elsewhere throughout this book we explore the many ways our overdependence on technology can hinder our ability to thrive. And as anyone with a phone knows, our ubiquitous screens are especially adept at sapping our attention. Multitasking with multiple devices has been shown to actually shrink our brains. The gray matter in an area of the brain called the anterior cingulate cortex, which is responsible for information processing, withers away. While we've been conditioned to believe we can't go even a few minutes without our phones, and that multitasking is our ticket to unlocking our superhuman productivity, it's time we understand just how self-defeating these beliefs can be.

What's fascinating is that multitasking also affects how we communicate and connect with others. We know our devices can be distracting when we're trying to talk to someone, but what's amazing is how our screens can affect us even when we're not using them. In a study by researchers at the University of Essex in the UK, participants were divided into couples and asked to talk. Half the conversations took place with a phone in the room. "The mere presence of mobile phones inhibited the development of interpersonal closeness and trust," the study contended, "and reduced the extent to which individuals felt empathy and understanding from their partners."

"LIFE IS LONG IF YOU KNOW HOW TO USE IT"

The relentless pace of life seems like a very modern phenomenon—and it's certainly a hallmark of our always-on culture—but the idea of choosing how we spend our time goes back to the ancients. They didn't have notifications pinging them every time a new email or text arrived, but they understood that our experience of time is what we make it. "It is not that we have a short time to live, but that we waste a lot of it," wrote the Roman philosopher Seneca. "Life is long enough, and a sufficiently generous amount has been given to us for the highest achievements if it were all well invested. . . . So it is: we are not given a short life but we make it short, and we are not ill-supplied but wasteful of it. . . . Life is long if you know how to use it."

That's some timeless wisdom! And yet, for many of us, days, weeks, and months can go by in what seems like the blink of an eye, and during that time it sometimes seems as though we've accomplished very little of real significance. That's why finding ways to focus on what's really meaningful—whether it's our family or goals and dreams that are close to our heart—is so valuable. That's something TEDx speaker, corporate chief communications officer, and executive coach Shira Miller discovered for herself. "My days were spent juggling a busy, full-time corporate job with starting to work on a book project I had shelved for years," said Miller, a master of multitasking (or so she thought) who firmly believed she was leading a good, full life. "I spent most weekends and nights creating a new website and building my social media presence, while continuing to rise at the crack of dawn for exercise, make time for my husband, and see friends."

The turning point came when Miller's eighty-year-old mother suffered a heart attack. "Overwhelmed, I suddenly couldn't think straight," Miller said. A session with her own coach led to the realization that she had to slow down. The upshot: Miller decided to make changes—prioritizing her time and energy. "I began prioritizing things one at a time rather than trying to do everything simultaneously. I cut back on business travel commitments and spent time with my mom instead, who is now fully recovered."

After implementing Microsteps, such as making a daily task list at work, Miller is now more realistic about what can be accomplished in a healthy manner. "I focus on the top five tasks each day and plan how much time is needed to accomplish

---

HOW I THRIVE

GRACE BYERS, actor

Focus on one thing at a time.

"I remind myself: 'How do you eat a (figurative) elephant? One bite at a time.' The time-sensitive, immediate things take priority and everything else takes a back seat until I'm able to handle them. My focus: one completed task at a time."

each one," Miller said. She also started to prioritize in a different way. For example, one day she'd been planning to devote time to writing and other creative projects, but Miller looked around and realized her cluttered home office was distracting her from focusing. So she spent the day organizing and clearing out folders of junk. "Making that one task my focus and taking the time to slowly and deliberately accomplish it was freeing," she said. "Plus, I eventually did everything else on my list more effectively."

A STRATEGIC START TO THE DAY

What happens in those first few hours after we wake has a substantial impact on the rest of our day. Those activities and events set the tone for everything to come. When you wake up, instead of reflexively starting your day by checking your messages, take a minute or so to breathe deeply. That breathing space can be expansive.

Even before you put your mind to work on the tasks of the day, remember to focus on yourself, to set the tone for the day in a positive way. That might mean meditating, working out, walking the dog, doing some stretching, or just drinking a cup of coffee in silence. The important thing to remember is that any morning routine you implement needs to be one that works well for you, according to how *your* mind and body function.

It's no surprise that many successful leaders take an intentional approach to how they start their day. According to Virgin Group chair Richard Branson, waking up early is a key to focus and productivity: "Like keeping a positive outlook, or keeping fit, waking up early is a habit, which you must work on to maintain . . ." he wrote in a blog. "I have learned that if I rise early I can achieve so much more in a day, and therefore in life."

For Oprah, the day starts with gratitude. "I wake up in the morning, and the first thing I say is 'thank you.' Even before I'm awake, even before my eyes are fully open. I say 'thank you.' I can feel the gratitude, like, 'I'm still here. I'm in a body. Thank you for that.'"

Once you've invested some time into nurturing your well-being, you can move on to thinking about your goals for the day. Here's one Microstep to try: simply write down your priorities for the day. Taking even a small amount of time to decide what's important and what's not can be key in reducing stress and improving productivity throughout the day. Early morning is also a good time for writing down your intentions that will support you in focusing on more ambitious, long-term projects as well.

YOUR ATTENTION IS A SUPERPOWER

Modern life has been structured so that we live in an almost permanent state of fight-or-flight. The demands and distractions just keep coming: another dozen emails calling out for a response, notifications and updates lighting up our phones, even well-intended interruptions that take our attention away from our priorities. According to a University of California, Irvine, study, it takes twenty-five minutes for us to return to our prior level of focus after being interrupted. Twenty-five minutes! We can't wave a magic wand and make it all disappear—nor would we necessarily want to—but by using Microsteps we can begin to liberate ourselves from the tyranny of our ever-expanding to-do lists.

When we truly focus, we reassert control over our time. Here's a Microstep to start with that really is too small to fail.

If there's something you need to do that will only take you two minutes, do it immediately. Finishing a quick task is often simpler than reviewing it, putting it in your calendar, and returning to it later.

It's all part of building your attention "muscle." Like any other muscle, our attention muscle needs to be exercised on a regular basis, says Thomas Oppong, founder of AllTopStartups and author of *Working in the Gig Economy*. Oppong notes that "while insignificant tasks requiring minimal cognitive effort can be performed in parallel, truly meaningful work requires a much more intense level of focus."

His suggestion: "Schedule blank space for intentional thinking to replenish your store of attention. Protect your time and manage your time like an investment portfolio." This might mean you'll disappoint others, many of whom believe their issue is worthy of your limited time. The truth is you can't meet every request from friends, family, and colleagues. As Oppong also advises, "Choose to be less reactive and more intentional about where you invest your attention. . . . Own your attention. A lack of ownership of attention can only make you waste precious time."

One way to own your attention is speaking up about it. Whether you're in an office, at home, or somewhere else, let others know that you are going into Do Not Disturb mode. It's a small way to protect your attention and your time—with fewer interruptions, you'll be better able to fully devote yourself to your project.

One of the most talked-about documentaries in 2020 was *The Social Dilemma*. It confronted some of the more troubling aspects of social media giants including Facebook, Twitter, and Instagram. The film features interviews with a range of experts, including many Silicon Valley insiders who helped create the monsters they are now warning about. As they see it, by mining data and manipulating human behavior, these tech platforms have turned our attention into one of the most valuable—and exploitable—commodities on the planet, with implications on everything from the future of democracy to our collective mental health.

One of the most trenchant critics is Tristan Harris, a former Google design ethicist who founded the group Time Well Spent to raise awareness about how our society is being "hijacked" by technology. As Harris points out, our addiction to our devices is by design. Behind those friendly, inviting icons we love so much is an incredible amount of increasingly

ATTENTION IS A FORM OF GIVING

To pay attention, this is our endless and proper work.

—Mary Oliver, American poet

sophisticated science. "The best way to get people's attention is to know how someone's mind works," says Harris. The behavioral scientists, neuroscientists, and computer scientists on the other side of our screens know we like the feeling of control. But they also want us to cede control of our attention. And so we're given the illusion of control. "By shaping the menus we pick from, technology hijacks the way we perceive our choices and replaces them with new ones," writes Harris. "But the closer we pay attention to the options we're given, the more we'll notice when they don't actually align with our true needs."

Since phone notifications are such frequent intruders on our attention, one of Harris's recommendations is to arrange to receive notifications only from people, not machines. Harris set his phone to ping him only from WhatsApp, iMessage, and other messaging services—instances where actual humans are on the other side requesting his attention. Any notifications coming from machines are turned off.

When we do this, a larger dishabituation happens. Minimizing all the buzzes "helps our mind get back control of itself," Harris says, since the more your phone buzzes, the more you'll expect it to buzz. "The less frequently our pocket's buzzing, the less our mind starts to feel those phantom buzzes in our pocket, and the calmer we get," he says. "Hopefully that helps you get back some control of your attention."

ONE THING AT A TIME

Building our attention muscle is not an end in itself. It opens us to so many benefits—including finding joy in whatever we're doing. As the British writer Alan Watts put it, "This is the real secret of life—to be completely engaged with what you are doing in the here and now. And instead of calling it work, realize it is play."

And the way to do it is to focus attentively, on one project at a time, with devotion. Again, the ancient philosophers knew this. Marcus Aurelius—the second-century Roman Emperor and author of *Meditations*—wrote about clearing the mind of distractions in order to focus on the most important task of the day, and how true wisdom and happiness come from taking action on things that most matter to you. "Do everything as if it were the last thing you were doing in your life," he said. A bit dramatic, perhaps, but his point is a good one: instead of always looking ahead to the next thing, and the next, there is something fundamentally meaningful about being in the present.

So here you are at your desk—or wherever you work—geared up to go. In all likelihood, there will be tasks you need to get done quickly. But you can still focus on your own priorities for the day, not based on what has most recently appeared in front of you, screaming for your attention, but on what matters most to you. One strategy: figure out when in the day you're most productive and plan to do your most challenging and meaningful work during that time.

If you're not convinced about the power of focus, conduct your own experiment: challenge yourself to work for an uninterrupted stretch on just one thing. Set a timer and don't allow yourself to be distracted for sixty to ninety minutes. You might be surprised at how much quality work you accomplish—and by how invigorated you feel at the end.

As we navigate the day it's often hard to know what's most important, partly because of endless incoming emails. According to a 2015 Adobe report, huge numbers of people are addicted to email, checking it around the clock—even in the bathroom! The researchers found the average white collar worker spends about six hours a day on email. Six hours! That doesn't leave much time for productive work, or, actually, anything else.

Rather than getting overwhelmed, get focused. One Microstep: take a daily tech time out to improve your focus and reduce stress. By setting aside time to step away from email, you'll be more available to truly connect with yourself and your loved ones.

The actor and investor Ashton Kutcher had the realization that emails were sapping his energy and time. Kutcher puts it like this: "Email is everyone else's to-do list for you. . . . I found myself waking up every day with 60, 70, 100 emails in my inbox

---

— HOW I THRIVE —

NILI LOTAN, fashion designer

Create a physical space that helps you focus.

"Find or create an environment for yourself to work where you feel safe, motivated, and empowered, whether it's a corner of your home, an office, your favorite chair."

• • • •

just from when I was sleeping. . . . By the time I got through I'd lost two hours of my morning to just responding to things, and it became this impossible hole to get out of."

Implementing simple Microsteps changed that pattern for Kutcher. "This is my journey that I'm on, and I want to choose when I'm available," he said. "The Do Not Disturb feature is actually really, really wonderful." Kutcher avoids checking email during the beginning of his workday. "When I wake up . . . I spend the first hour of my work not looking at email, and actually just writing out what it is that I want to accomplish in a given day," Kutcher said. "And then before I go through my emails, I'll do all my outgoing, outbound stuff, which is what I want everyone else to do for me. And then I'll go and get reactive to whatever's going on."

COMPLETE A PROJECT BY DROPPING IT

We all have projects lined up, whether they're personal or work-related: books we've always said we'd read, languages we feel we ought to learn, courses to take that will bring us new skills and strengthen our resumes.

These unfinished (and often unstarted) projects can weigh us down over time. Often, we load ourselves up with goals we think we *should* aspire to, even if we don't really. We take on too much and then judge ourselves harshly when we don't do what we set out to do. It can come down to things we may not even want to do—but have taken on because of other people's expectations, or due to unrealistic expectations of our own.

So if there's an activity or half-hearted ambition in your life that's draining your energy and keeping you from what really matters, consider letting it go. When you give yourself permission to cut loose the things you don't really care about, you'll have more time and energy left for what you really value. That's what Arianna found when she did a "life audit" at the age of forty.

> I realized how many projects I had committed to in my head—such as learning German and becoming a good skier and learning to cook. Most remained unfinished, and many were not even started. Yet these countless incomplete projects drained my energy and diffused my attention. As soon as the file was opened, each one took a little bit of me away. It was very liberating to realize that I could "complete" a project by simply dropping it—by eliminating it from my to-do list. Why carry around this unnecessary baggage? That's how I completed learning German and becoming a good skier and learning to cook and a host of other projects that now no longer have a claim on my attention.

PRIORITIZE YOU

Focusing on yourself to personally enhance your own life is not self-serving. In fact, taking care of yourself leads to greater fulfillment so you have more time, energy, and space in your life for others. According to the entrepreneur Tim Ferriss, "There's a difference between being selfish and putting yourself first. . . . If you don't take care of yourself and your own needs, you'll find you have increasingly little of yourself to give—both to your own priorities and to projects for the people in your life whom you want to help."

When we do take care of ourselves, we're far better able to focus, set priorities, and pursue our own version of success—not someone else's. A 2018 study published in the journal *Frontiers in Psychology* found that exercising regularly improves our ability to focus. Even a few minutes of silence—just being instead of doing—is restorative and far from a waste of time. As the seventeenth-century French mathematician and philosopher Blaise Pascal put it, "All of humanity's problems stem from man's inability to sit quietly in a room alone."

Research shows that meditators indeed experience less mind wandering—which improves concentration. Silence can actually cultivate new cells in the hippocampus, the part of the brain responsible for memory and storing information, according to a study in the journal *Brain Structure and Function*.

Meditation also helps us to refocus after being distracted—an increasingly common peril of our technology-besieged lives. Giuseppe Pagnoni, a neuroscientist at Emory University, found that, after an interruption, participants who meditated were able to return to what they had been focusing on faster than nonmeditators. "The regular practice of meditation may enhance the capacity to limit the influence of distracting thoughts," he said.

In today's world, in which our work follows us everywhere, prioritizing meditation exercises and self-care activities may sound difficult—but, as with everything else, you can take Microsteps to help you set priorities and focus on what really matters.

· · ·

MICROSTEP DIARY

Kirsten Harman, project manager

MICROSTEP: Set aside five minutes each day to meditate.

Why I Chose It

We all know the many benefits of meditation, from helping to reduce stress and anxiety (which I experience on a daily basis) to improving sleep and focus (also areas I struggle in). I wanted to create a morning routine that begins with meditating for five minutes instead of checking social media. By checking social media in the morning, I end up staying in bed for longer and then feel rushed. I start the day focused on what other people are up to instead of giving myself time to reflect and set my day up for success.

What Happened

Instead of reaching for my phone I let some light into my room, took a few deep breaths, and got out of bed. After washing my face and drinking water, I settled down on my couch for my five-minute meditation. I've started with the Basics pack on Headspace. After meditating a few days in a row, I definitely noticed a difference in my mood. On Sunday, I started the day by checking my phone in bed and meditated at night instead, and I did not feel as great throughout the day.

Out of the thirty-two days, I completed my Microstep twenty-five times. I saw an almost immediate difference in my stress levels when I started my day meditating versus checking my phone. By taking a few minutes to focus on myself each morning, I was able to go into the day with a clear mind. I plan to keep up my Microstep, but even if I don't have time to meditate, I still plan to not look at my phone and take a few deep breaths before starting my day.

MICROSTEPS

In the morning, write down your priorities for the day. Deciding what's important and what's not is key to reducing stress and improving productivity.

Take a minute to block off time for focused work today—ideally in the morning. Set a calendar reminder and let colleagues know so they'll be less likely to interrupt you. Researchers have suggested that 75–120 minutes of focus time is optimal for productivity, but if that's too ambitious, even 30 minutes will make a difference.

If something takes less than two minutes, do it immediately. Finishing a quick task is often simpler than reviewing it, putting it in your calendar, and returning to it later.

Make at least one meeting each day device-free. You'll be more focused, engaged, and productive, and your team will be more creative without distractions from phones and computers.

At the start of every virtual meeting, close out of any chat programs or email windows. It's easy to get distracted by notifications. You'll be more focused and productive (and more respectful of the meeting organizer) if you give the meeting your full attention, the way you would in person.

Set time on your calendar to manage your email each day. Studies show that it takes an average of twenty-five minutes to refocus after being interrupted, so setting aside time for email can help you avoid constant inbox distractions.

Take a daily tech time out to improve your focus and reduce stress. Set aside time to step away from social media and email so you can truly connect with yourself and your loved ones.

Log off from remote work at the same time you typically leave the office. It's important to build in time at night to rest and recharge so you can work sustainably.

Let go of something today that you no longer need. Think about something that is draining your energy without benefiting you or anyone you love: resentments, negative self-talk, a project you know you are not really going to complete, anything. And then let it go.

Set aside five minutes each day to meditate. When you calm your mind and shut out outside noises and distractions, you'll return to your work ready to focus and produce.

Once a day, schedule time for deep work and let others know you need to focus. Be vocal about going into Do Not Disturb mode: time for focused work, without interruption, preferably in a quiet place. You'll be more productive at the office and less likely to have a lot of work you must complete at night.

HOW YOU CAN THRIVE

What are some moments and situations throughout the day when you find yourself distracted?

What are the environmental factors that make it difficult for you to focus?

Are there certain limiting beliefs you have that negatively impact your ability to focus? For example, *I'll never get everything done unless I multitask* or *It's impossible for me to set priorities since everything is always changing.*

Did any of the science or stories in this chapter help you think differently about how to set priorities and build your attention muscle?

What's one Microstep you can implement that will help you minimize distractions and sharpen your focus?

6

• • •

COMMUNICATION
AND RELATIONSHIPS

*S*o much of our twenty-first century understanding of communication and connection is centered on technology. In our daily
swirl of emails, texts, calls, and video conferences, it's easy to minimize the human element—and even easier when staying safe and
healthy requires us to keep our distance. As amazing as our devices
and innovations may be, it's other people who are our greatest resources when it comes to living a thriving life. It's why I've always
sworn by the importance of having a support group of family and
friends to give me honest feedback and to support me when the going
gets tough, and, just as important, to help me celebrate and appreciate the good times too.

Whether we're interacting through cutting-edge technology or
in a more old-fashioned, face-to-face way, our relationships with
others can be among the richest and most rewarding parts of our
lives. And each of us has an extraordinary capacity to connect with
others in ways that can yield big results on everything from our
well-being and performance to our happiness and creativity.

I was blessed to have a mother who was incapable of having an impersonal relationship with anyone. If the FedEx man arrived to drop off a package, my mom—or Yaya, as everyone called her— would have him come in, sit down at the kitchen table, and offer him something to eat. If you went to the farmers market with my mother, or to a department store, you'd better be prepared for a long discussion with the shop assistant or the farmer about their lives before she even got around to asking about something she wanted to buy. That intimacy with strangers, that empathy toward everyone she encountered, was something I had been surrounded with since I was a little girl in Athens.

Whatever stage of life we're in, however busy we are, our ability to communicate and connect with family, friends, colleagues, and even strangers is a foundation of our well-being. Even if it doesn't come as naturally as it did to my mother, there are Microsteps we can take to strengthen and sustain these bonds. When we do, we open ourselves to new experiences and perspectives that make our journey immeasurably richer.

—Arianna Huffington

• • • •

HUMAN BEINGS ARE hardwired to connect. Our relationships with others—from friends and family to partners and coworkers—are in many ways the foundation of our lives. And our ability to build, nurture, and maintain these relationships can have a big impact on our ability to thrive.

We intuitively know that happy relationships can improve our lives, but this was conclusively validated by an eighty-year-long Harvard study on happiness that began tracking students back in 1938. "It turns out that people who are more socially connected to family, to friends, to community, are happier, they're physically healthier, and they live longer than people who are less well connected," Robert Waldinger, the director of the study, said in his 2015 TED Talk about the findings.

Research also tells us what can happen when we lack meaningful relationships. Studies show that loneliness, for example, is a risk factor for a range of mental and physical health issues, including heart disease and stroke, depression, and even increased mortality. And then, as we've already explored, we're more connected than ever before through our devices, but all too often we are disconnected from those who matter most. But with the right set of tools, we have more power than we realize to strengthen our connections and build relationships that fuel our well-being, performance, and sense of purpose.

> **HOW I THRIVE**
>
> **MARY DILLON**, CEO of Ulta Beauty
>
> ### Ask a friend or coworker at least one question a day.
>
> "Show curiosity. It is surprising how much you can learn about people—and comfortable you can make them—by simply asking about them. And, if someone doesn't ask questions in return—it tells you a lot! Just sayin'."

DE AMICITIA

The meaning and connection we derive from other people is one of the bedrock truths going back to ancient times. Aristotle, for instance, wrote in the *Nicomachean Ethics* about the nature of friendship, distinguishing between friendships based on utility or pleasure and deeper friendships rooted in shared values. In 44 BC, the Roman statesman and philosopher Marcus Tullius Cicero wrote *De Amicitia* (*How to Be a Friend*). Among his timeless insights are that friends challenge us to be better people ("Even when a friend is absent, he is still present") and that, for all the benefits it brings us, "The reward of friendship is friendship itself."

Whatever kind of relationships we have or aspire to have, we can take small steps to make them more meaningful and fulfilling—and we can even learn to spot opportunities for connection we didn't see before.

How do we do it? We start small. Instead of starting an exchange by sharing your opinion, ask the other person to share theirs. Ask a question. Turn a transactional moment into something more—when you're at your favorite coffee place making your usual order, or dialing into a call center to get tech support, take the opportunity to make a human connection. When we examine our habits, we may be surprised at how wrapped up in ourselves we can be, how many barriers we've erected. And we may be equally surprised at how easy it is to shift gears and genuinely connect.

This kind of connection is only possible when we pay attention to someone else. That sounds obvious, but think of all the obstacles to paying attention we encounter on any given day. If we are distracted by our devices, or always thinking ahead to whatever deadline or task is causing us stress, we're likely to miss the moment. If we consider ourselves too busy for other people because time spent getting to know others feels unproductive and takes us away from what feels urgent, we may find ourselves suffering from loneliness, a growing epidemic.

In *Together: The Healing Power of Human Connection in a Sometimes Lonely World*, Vivek Murthy, a former surgeon general, notes that loneliness is one of the biggest challenges affecting people from all walks of life. And every interaction we have can fuel our well-being. As Murthy writes, "'Relational energy' refers to the emotional energy generated (or depleted) in every social interaction." Citing research from the University of Michigan's Center for Positive Organizations, Murthy demonstrates that relational energy can have multiple benefits. First, we have an emotional reaction "when we feel good making a strong positive connection with another person." That's not so surprising.

HOW I THRIVE

KIMBERLY PERRY, musician

When you feel overwhelmed, tell someone you trust instead of holding your emotions in.

"I've always been somebody who felt like they really had it together. And it was hard to not have it together at all in those moments—but it was so helpful to talk to the people around me. . . . Vulnerability was very important for me: communication with a vulnerable and open heart."

● ● ● ●

But that emotional positivity ignites a cognitive reaction that provides benefits to our memory and cognitive performance: "In short, connection often makes us feel better emotionally, which fires up our engagement with the tasks in front of us. And when we're energized and engaged at work, it leads to the third reaction—productivity."

With these benefits in mind, we have an immediate opportunity to shift our mindset. Instead of viewing each day as predictable, we can see hundreds of potential connections. When we are willing to be surprised by others, learn from them, and expand ourselves in the process, we open the door to new experiences and perspectives—and make each day a lot more interesting.

APPRECIATING THOSE CLOSEST TO US

Here's another tip from the ancients. As Marcus Aurelius advised, focusing on the positive qualities of our loved ones can lift our own spirits in an instant. "When you want to cheer yourself up, think of the good qualities of those you live with. For instance, the energy of one, the modesty of another, the generosity of a third, and so on. For nothing gives us as much pleasure as seeing the examples of the virtues presented in abundance by those who live among us. Therefore keep them always near at hand."

It's not only about us; we can acknowledge our appreciation through small acts of kindness in any relationship, whether it's a new acquaintance or a life partner. Matthew Siedhoff, vice chair for gynecology at Cedars-Sinai in Los Angeles, leaves his partner a handwritten note by the coffeemaker every morning. "The message is simple—something funny, a little encouragement, sometimes an apology, always an expression of love. My therapist taught me these actions make deposits in the 'relationship bank,' filling up our reserves so we can better weather the difficult times," he told Thrive Global.

These tiny gestures add up. Couples who are generous with each other are far more likely to report very happy marriages, according to the University of Virginia's National Marriage Project. Generosity, in this case, is about doing more than what we're expected to do as a spouse or partner—even something as mundane as doing housework. "Generosity is going above and beyond the ordinary expectations with small acts of service and making an extra effort to be affectionate," said W. Bradford Wilcox, a sociologist who led the research.

Another way to boost the quality of our most important relationships is to do fun, novel activities together, and to do them frequently. The endeavor doesn't have to be expensive or time-consuming. It can be something as simple as trying a new coffee spot together, or taking a brief walk after dinner, or waking up a pinch earlier to watch the sun come up. For romantic relationships, research published in the *Journal of Personality and Social Psychology* confirms that doing self-expanding activities together—things that feel exciting or different or help us see ourselves in a new way—can even increase sexual desire in long-term partners. Having new experiences together can "spark some of the feelings of desire and excitement from the early stages of relationships," the researchers said, "feelings that may be harder to recall for couples who are in longer compared with shorter relationships."

THE POWER OF LISTENING

No matter what the relationship, long-term or fleeting, our ability to listen is one of the most valuable skills we have as human beings. "We have two ears and one mouth, so we should listen more than we say," Zeno of Citium (334–262 BC) is believed to have said. And indeed, the founder of Stoicism was onto something all those centuries ago. Listening is what allows us to understand, empathize, and build meaningful relationships with others. Active listening, or deep listening, is at the heart of every thriving relationship. The term *active listening*, coined in 1957 by American psychologists Carl Rogers and Richard Farson, means that we, as listeners, are engaged members of a conversation—but we don't do much speaking. Unlike a verbal listener, or someone who "listens to respond," an active listener will ask questions when appropriate and maintain nonverbal involvement, like nodding their head or keeping eye contact.

Some people are naturally good at this form of listening, like Joe-Annis Iodice, a Florida-based Lyft driver in her seventies. To her, active listening is part of the job description. While some riders prefer silence, many of the people who slide into her back seat can sense she's an adept listener, and they will start talking right away. And when they do, Iodice practices stillness, which is different from being quiet. "Being quiet means you could be waiting for the other person to stop speaking so you can say what it is you want to say," she told Thrive Global. "But being *still* is being able to really absorb what the other person is saying." Stillness, by her definition, provides us with the mental clarity to give a thoughtful response, when and if it becomes appropriate to speak (more on this later). We can take Microsteps to practice stillness on our own so that we can become better at it when we're with other people. We might consider going for a walk with no headphones, or taking just a few minutes each day to meditate. When we make time to practice stillness, we'll be better prepared as a listener to focus on what's right in front of us.

This form of listening really works. A study published in the *International Journal of Listening* shows that when people were met with active listening, they felt more understood than participants who received either advice or simple acknowledgments. It's a truth that can bruise the ego of some self-identifying "good" listeners—those who give unsolicited

---

HOW I THRIVE

JENNY TEGROTENHUIS,
LMHC, The Gottman Institute relationship therapist

Be specific with your praise.

"Be like a mirror, and let your partner know exactly what you see, feel, and experience about them that is beautiful. 'I love your voice, the shape of your hands, how good you are with money, etc.' Let your partner know exactly how happy you are to be with them. We never get tired of knowing we're valued and cherished. Gottman research shows that the happiest couples communicate genuine admiration and appreciation toward their partners every day."

• • • •

advice, or say they know *exactly* how we feel, or point out just how much worse things could be, which are all responses that can minimize the other person's feelings. We've all done this at one point or another, but by making small adjustments we can shift to the kind of active listening that can lead to truly interesting places.

In addition to practicing nonverbal acknowledgment, we can model "person-centered therapy," a technique pioneered by Carl Rogers, one of the aforementioned psychologists. When speaking with patients, Rogers would mirror back what his clients were saying, without offering any advice. We don't need to be therapists to practice this in real time, but we can do it with Microsteps. For example, once a day, try having a conversation where you mostly listen. When you do speak, make sure it's not to insert your opinion but to invite the other person to go deeper.

Remembering small details is also a great way to demonstrate active listening. As a bartender in New York City, Tess Jonas naturally listens to and remembers certain guests' orders. There's one patron, she says, who has dined alone at

---

HOW I THRIVE

VERNĀ MYERS, VP of inclusion strategy, Netflix

Think of criticisms as information, not attacks.

"If someone is kind enough to share with you the impact of your statement on them, see it as a gift. See it as an opportunity to maybe change something—maybe it was the tone of your voice, or maybe it's what you said before you said that thing—but the person is giving you information. Consider it an opportunity to grow."

● ● ●

the bar a few times during dinner rush hour, and *always* orders a Coca-Cola, a filet, fries, and a side of tomatoes. "Are you sure you don't want the Campari tomatoes too?" she asked him the one time his order was different. He was touched by this gesture, and he texted his wife, "The bartender remembers me." The next time you're talking with a friend, listen for what's coming up in their week and remember the details—maybe they're particularly stressed about an event. Then, later on, follow up with them to see how it went. You may be surprised how simply showing you were paying attention can strengthen your bond.

One of the things that makes it harder and harder to be an effective listener today is our increasing dependence on technology. A 2017 study found that the mere presence of a phone nearby—even if it's facedown, on silent, or in our bag or pocket—limits our available cognitive capacity and functioning, even though we may feel we're fully focused and attentive. Experts call it brain drain. (For more on how our relationship with technology affects our personal relationships, check out Chapter 2.)

HOW TO APPROACH CONFLICT

Conflict in relationships is inevitable, even healthy. In fact, the absence of conflict can be a sign of an unhealthy relationship or a bond that's gone stale, according to research from John Gottman, a psychological researcher and clinician who has studied love and marriage for over forty years. (Incidentally, Gottman believes Microsteps are key for lasting relationships: "Successful long-term relationships are created through small words, small gestures, and small acts," he has said.) How we approach disagreement in our personal lives can either destroy our relationships or help them thrive. With Microsteps, like taking a single deep breath before we deliver critical feedback, we can improve how we communicate when things get tough.

It's normal to become impassioned when we discuss something personal. In fact, emotional intensity can be a sign of sincerity, Kristin Behfar, a professor of strategic leadership and ethics at the United States Army War College, told Thrive Global. It's when we become hostile that the other person may shut down and stop processing whatever it is we have to say. When we recognize that our emotions are running high, a simple way to course-correct is to name the specific emotion that we feel. We can say "I know I'm being intense right now" or "I recognize that I feel very strongly about this." This verbal acknowledgment can help the other person to depersonalize what might otherwise come off as an attack, Behfar says.

And while it's normal to become emotional in the face of conflict, waiting until you're out of a heated moment is a key to giving feedback, Eve Rodsky, a lawyer, organizational management specialist, and author of *Fair Play*, a book and card system encouraging a more fair division of household labor, told Thrive. "Behavioral economist Dan Ariely was an expert I interviewed for *Fair Play*. And we talked a lot about emotional cascades, when you're spiraling," Rodsky said. "What happens when you're communicating during an emotional cascade? You may say things like, 'Fine, I'm never taking out the trash again.' And then do you hold to that? If you say, 'I'm not going with you to Disneyland,' then do you not go to Disneyland? Do you stubbornly hold on to poor decisions because you're holding on to what you said during your cascade? Don't give feedback in the moment. Schedule a check-in time, whether it's with your boss or with your partner. That's where you'll talk best—when you're both calm, and you're not experiencing an emotional cascade."

When discussing a specific point of conflict with a partner, friend, or coworker, another widely effective strategy is to stick to "I" instead of "you" statements. Accusations can create a vicious cycle of blame, while expressing our own feelings opens up a conversation. For example, instead of saying to a friend, "You're never on time," you can try saying, "I feel unimportant when you're late to our dinner plans."

An apology is one of the most powerful ways to resolve, or at least address, a conflict. Apologizing to someone when we've wronged them is essential to keeping the relationship intact, but it's not always as simple as saying sorry. An effective apology is best done in person, Lauren Bloom, author of *Art of the Apology: How, When, and Why to Give and Accept Apologies*, told Thrive Global. But if a face-to-face conversation isn't possible, a phone call or video chat are great alternatives. While we have the other person's attention, Bloom suggests taking responsibility for the harm we caused ("I shouldn't have

> ——— HOW I THRIVE ———
> **ANGELA SANTOMERO**,
> television producer
>
> **Encourage someone you don't know well to tell you their story.**
>
> "My favorite way to connect is to dig deeper and connect more to find out everyone's story. This has changed the way I view small talk—it's to talk to fewer people in a deeper way. "
>
> • • • •

done that") and making amends as best as we can ("What can I do to fix it?"). It can also be helpful to express what we value about the other person, why they are a friend we want to keep. Then, one of the most vital ingredients to the apology isn't about the apology at all, it's about your behavior moving forward. When we hear it, it sounds rather obvious, but it's a step that many of us skip: Don't do the upsetting thing again. If it's a behavior that feels baked into your personality, you can intentionally take a Microstep to help you improve. For example, people who are chronically late can set plans on their calendar for fifteen to twenty minutes earlier than they need to, essentially tricking themselves into being on time.

This may come as a relief: not all relationship problems can be solved, nor should they be! About 70 percent of problems that couples face in their relationship fall into the "perpetual problems" category, according to research from The Gottman Institute. By definition, they are problems that don't have a clear resolution. Unlike solvable problems,

---

HOW I THRIVE

GREG LUTZE, founder of social media app VSCO

Every day, make an effort to speak to someone older or younger than you.

"Around 75 percent of the people on VSCO are under the age of 25, and I get the opportunity to talk to them often. I am constantly surprised by their outlook on life and desire for positive social change—particularly around respecting people and caring for the environment. It's easy to discount teenagers and their perspective on life, but really, there is so much to learn from them."

like someone falling behind on their household chores and the other person picking up the slack, perpetual problems have to do with the composition of who we are as individual people. These compositions are often related to personality or lifestyle differences, like one partner requiring a more active social life than the other. There's nothing inherently wrong with perpetual problems; we sign up for them when we enter into relationships with people who don't match our exact social DNA. They're only worrisome when we become obsessed with solving them. According to Gottman, our ability to have a healthy dialogue about these problems is more important than actually arriving at a solution. Instead of trying to solve the problem, we can ask ourselves, "How can I better understand their perspective?"

This measured approach, as the ancients well knew, can also prevent us from falling into resentment and grudge-holding. The Stoic philosopher Seneca wrote: "How much better to heal than seek revenge from injury. Vengeance wastes a lot of time and exposes you to many more injuries than the first that sparked it. Anger always outlasts hurt. Best to take the opposite course. Would anyone think it normal to return a kick to a mule or a bite to a dog?"

HOW "WEAK TIES" CAN STRENGTHEN OUR WELL-BEING

As children, we're told we shouldn't talk to strangers. But as we grow, learning to interact with people unlike ourselves, even in small and seemingly insignificant ways, can be one of our richest sources of connection. This becomes especially important as common experiences, such as the COVID-19 pandemic, make clear just how interconnected we really are.

When we approach other people with this mindset, we see that the barriers that separate us—or that we've been *told* separate us—aren't so hard to get past. If our eyes pass over someone because of a snap judgment, or because we deem them to be not like us, we may miss an opportunity to connect with someone whose experience and perspective might teach us something, or open us up. The actress Teri Hatcher says talking to strangers about "anything and everything, big and small" is her secret life hack. She talks to the person in line next to her at the grocery store and engages with someone in a clothing store about women's body issues. "I think by talking to people, being connected, you realize you are part of a community and that people are all just trying to do their best. We are a lot more similar than we are different and that gives me peace and hope," she told Thrive.

These little connections can yield big returns. Decades of research show that casual relationships, or "weak ties"—a term coined by sociologist Mark Granovetter in a 1973 paper—have a significant positive impact on well-being. Weak ties are the low-stakes relationships in our lives, like the one we may have with our local barista, dry cleaner, or former coworker. "Taking a few minutes to engage with people we see regularly or joining a group—such as a religious group, a sports team or a hobby meetup—has been shown to increase our satisfaction with life," Allie Volpe writes in a *New York Times* article, "Why You Need a Network of Low-Stakes, Casual Friendships."

A 2014 study, for example, found that the more weak ties a person has, the happier they feel. Weak ties can even improve physical health, according to a 2019 study from the

University of Texas at Austin. The study included more than three hundred adults over the age of sixty-five, and researchers found that those who socialized with not just their family and close friends but also with acquaintances and even strangers were more likely to have higher levels of physical activity.

In another two-part study examining the link between weak ties and well-being, researchers found that people who, on average, have more daily weak-tie interactions than others, or who have more weak-tie interactions than they're used to, report feeling happier and a greater sense of belonging. Weak ties can't replace the role of intimate relationships—but they can harmonize. "People with high levels of what psychologists call social integration—those who participate in a broad range of relationships that consist of both intimate and weak ties—tend to be healthier and happier," the *Washington Post* reports.

And then, a relationship that begins as a weak tie may lead to something more, as it did for Harvard professor and positive

---

HOW I THRIVE

JULIANNE HOLT-LUNSTAD, psychologist

Every day, make an effort to get to know someone new.

"My general recommendation is to start taking social relationships seriously, for the sake of your health. We now have strong evidence that our social connections have a significant impact on our health and longevity, comparable to the effects of things that we take quite seriously, like obesity. So it's time to start paying attention to our social relationships the same way we pay attention to our diet and exercise."

---

psychologist Tal Ben-Shahar. In his 2018 book, *Short Cuts to Happiness: Life-Changing Lessons from My Barber*, Ben-Shahar reflects on the impact that Avi, his Israeli neighborhood hair stylist, had on his life and the lives of many others. "Avi's salon is a gathering place that provides women, men, and children living in the neighborhood much more than a hairdo. His relaxed manner and generous hospitality, his wit and wisdom, affords people just what the fast-paced, high-tech, postmodern world lacks," he writes, speaking to the power of what once were weak-tie relationships that, when they harmonize, can strengthen an entire community.

For many of us, one of the biggest challenges of the COVID-19 pandemic has been missing other people—being with the ones we love, meeting new people, even doing things that once annoyed us like waiting in long lines or being in crowds. As we've been forced to pause these interactions and endure long periods of isolation, we've had an opportunity to reflect on how interconnected we really are—and recognize that our most nourishing relationships are something we should never take for granted.

FORGING MEANINGFUL RELATIONSHIPS AT WORK

For many of us, work might not spring to mind as a top source of meaningful relationships. But with the average full-time American employee spending about forty-three hours per week at work, it's one of the best places to get the recommended six hours per day (yes, six hours!) of social contact. Unfortunately, it's also the place where many people tend to fall short in making friends.

When Gallup surveyed more than fifteen million employees around the world, less than a third reported having a best friend at work. The researchers used the specific phrase "best friend" because earlier studies had suggested best friends were a greater predictor of workplace outcomes than even a "good friend" at work, but we see now that any form of meaningful connection in the workplace is beneficial for our well-being. (If you prefer to keep your workplace relationships more formal, and it's working well for you, that's okay too!) Research shows that forming friendly work relationships can also increase our happiness, foster a sense of community, and even impact job performance. People with work friends are seven times as likely to be engaged in their work, and they have higher levels of retention than those who don't.

Even so, work friendships can be a thorny terrain. We may fear being vulnerable or appearing unprofessional. Those in leadership or managerial roles may struggle with this more, as they question whether they should be authoritative or congenial. The good news is that it's possible to be both. We can build trust, empathy, and authenticity while still being seen as a leader. In fact, these traits are essential to strong leadership. Without trust, for example, our team may not perform at their best. And according to a recent Gallup report, employees are 70 percent less likely to report burnout if they feel supported by their manager, and employees who say their supervisor is always willing to listen to their work-related problems are 62 percent less likely to be burned out.

PHRASES TO STOP SAYING—AND
WHAT TO SAY INSTEAD

Some phrases are so baked into corporate culture that we use them without thinking of their impact. For example, the ubiquitous email opener "Gentle reminder" rarely feels gentle. In fact, it often feels stressful, and so it runs counter to compassionate directness. Instead, try being clear and direct. Joseph A. DeVito, author of *The Interpersonal Communication Book*, recommends saying "I completely understand that you've got a lot on your plate, but I need to hear back from you on this today."

While you're here, consider swapping these unhelpful phrases as well:

Stop saying: "Does that make sense?"
Here's why: The question implies that the listener doesn't have the capacity to understand what you're saying, or the agency to ask for clarity on their own.
Try this instead: "What additional information would be helpful to you?"

Stop saying: "That's a no-brainer."
Here's why: It can destructively imply that any thought to the contrary is wrong, which makes it challenging for others to surface problems with openness and creativity.
Try this instead: "That makes sense to me."

Stop saying: "As most of you already know . . ."
Here's why: It can feel disparaging to listeners who weren't informed, causing them to question their worth: *If most people know about this, why don't I?*
Try this instead: Drop the precursor and just say what you have to say, even if you have a hunch that other people are aware of your announcement.

For leaders and employees alike, the process of giving feedback can further complicate workplace relationships. But when delivered in a certain way, feedback can not only help others improve, but it can also strengthen your relationship in important ways. Feedback, after all, is how we improve and get better. There's nothing wrong with failure or mistakes. They're inevitable. The key is to learn from mistakes and failures in order to avoid them in the future. And ignoring them or not giving employees honest, constructive feedback isn't polite, it's disrespectful—it doesn't acknowledge their potential or help them reach it.

That's why at Thrive we believe in compassionate directness. It's number one on our list of cultural values, and we teach it to other companies as well. Compassionate directness empowers employees to speak up, give feedback, and disagree, surface problems and pain points, and offer constructive criticism. And we encourage employees to do this immediately, continuously, and with clarity, but with compassion, empathy, and understanding. With compassionate directness as the foundation of a company's culture, both the employees and the business can course-correct, overcome challenges, grow, evolve, reach their highest potential, and truly thrive.

A key component of compassionate directness, and for effective communication in the workplace more broadly, is to be mindful of when a conversation should be had face-to-face versus over email or some other messaging tool. Before sending off a message, perform a Microstep to consider its appropriateness. Simply ask yourself: Will this note be better received if I deliver it in person (or face-to-face on a video call)? If you're communicating something that has the potential to be taken out of context, or is just too nuanced, the answer is likely yes. If so, then it may be worth pivoting and having the conversation face-to-face. If that isn't possible, consider picking up the phone and dialing the other person. As one study published in the *Journal of Experimental Social Psychology* found, a live exchange is thirty-four times more likely to be met with a positive response than one that happens over email.

Being compassionately direct with our teammates is indeed a form of kindness, a way of showing them that we care about them. It's a skill that takes time to master, but the more we flex those muscles, the more innate it becomes, and the greater profits it can yield. In addition to sharing your honest feedback, one Microstep is to actually ask for honest feedback from others. Frame the question as "What's one thing I could do differently to better support you?" instead of just asking if they have any feedback. They'll be more likely to respond with honesty when you make it clear that you want to grow and improve.

Jeremy Berman, a CEO and cofounder of Dream See Do, recently saw the benefits for himself when a team member approached him about his tendency to micromanage.

"I was so appreciative that he had the self-awareness to notice this, the bravery and emotional intelligence to address this head-on and immediately, and the sensitivity to be honest and firm, yet clear and unthreatening in his approach," Berman told Thrive Global. "I reached back out to him to clear the air, letting him know what my intention was, and that I would work to be more clear with a similar situation in the future. I feel like it was an immense learning experience for us both! We both see ourselves as progressive, lifelong learners who are continuously working on our own 'stuff' and practicing our emotional intelligence, and this is one example where that worked beautifully in practice."

To practice mindful communication at work immediately, try pausing to reflect before giving someone feedback—whether in-person or by text or email. Our devices make it so easy to fire off a response before we've even considered how our message might be received. If we're stressed or rushed, we're more likely to deliver feedback without compassion or empathy—even if that's unintentional. Also, instead of hoping a problem will go away, or assuming someone else will fix it, we can practice compassionate directness by surfacing an issue as soon as we notice it rather than letting it fester. When we speak up with clarity and empathy, everyone—including ourselves—benefits.

· · · ·

MICROSTEP DIARY

Summer Mattice, director of customer success

MICROSTEP: Set aside just a few minutes each night to write in a journal.

Why I Chose It

With our lives moving at the speed of light, I wanted to take concerted time to slow down to the pace of handwriting, to take time to reflect, and to capture all the wonderful crazy things we may otherwise lose over time. When I started, I hoped to build a habit that I'd continue doing as part of my nighttime routine.

What Happened

Overall I think this experiment was very successful! I think this was largely due to attaching my Microstep to a clear, important purpose in my life. Instead of reflecting on my life at large, I turned the journal into a daily note for my partner, which I'm planning to share with him as a gift, capturing small moments in our relationship that we may have otherwise forgotten. While I still received the positive benefits of keeping the journal, setting a specific intention for it was what really kept me on track. It also centered me and brought my brain speed down from typing to writing—a lovely slowdown.

MICROSTEPS

During your day make a personal connection with people you might normally tend to pass by and take for granted. It might be a checkout clerk or someone in your neighborhood you've never met. See how this helps you feel more alive and reconnected to the moment.

Start your next conversation with a question about the other person. Approach the person with genuine curiosity. What might you learn from them? How might they inspire you?

Today, share constructive feedback with one coworker. Start with "I care about you, and that's why I want to give you my honest feedback." Compassionate directness helps us build trust and surface issues before they become problems.

Ask a trusted friend for their compassionately direct feedback. Sometimes our impact on others doesn't match up with our intentions. Receiving honest feedback may hurt at first, but consider it a valuable opportunity to build self-awareness.

Once a day, have a conversation where you mostly listen. Don't underestimate the power of silence. Instead of giving your opinion or changing the subject, invite the other person to go deeper.

Next time you're tempted to criticize someone else, pause for one breath to reflect before you speak. In the heat of the moment, you're more likely to deliver your message without compassion or empathy—even if that's unintentional.

When giving someone feedback about something that upset you, raise the issue using "I" instead of "you." Accusations create a vicious cycle of blame, but expressing your own feelings opens up a conversation. Instead of "You never do what you're supposed to do," try "I feel stressed when I come home and the tasks haven't been done." Using "I" statements also helps us to feel empowered.

Each week, schedule some one-on-one time with your partner. Visit your favorite restaurant, whip something up in your own kitchen, or curl up on the couch together. By making alone time a priority, you'll create the space for meaningful conversations to be had and special memories to be made.

The next time you connect with a colleague, swap "How are you?" for a deeper question. Questions like "What's on your mind?" or "What challenges are you facing now?" can give you the chance to learn about and honor their experiences.

Ask someone with a different perspective for feedback on a project you're working on. Looking outside your own experience is a great way to illuminate any blind spots and see your work and its impact from a different angle.

HOW YOU CAN THRIVE

What are some situations in life and work where you're not able to communicate as meaningfully and authentically as you would like?

What are three relationships in your life you wish you could strengthen—with friends, family, coworkers, anyone?

What are some limiting beliefs you have that hold you back from building quality relationships or communicating effectively? For example, *I'm shy* or *I'm too busy and stressed to make time for deep conversations.*

Did any of the science or stories in this chapter help you think differently about connecting with others? How so?

What's one Microstep you read that will help you feel more meaningfully connected? Who in your life do you plan to implement it with?

7

· · · ·

CREATIVITY AND INSPIRATION

*T*he notion of creativity has a sense of magic and mystery about it. But this magic and mystery can make the very idea of creativity seem distant and unattainable. From awe-inspiring works of art that stir our souls to innovative ideas that change the world, creativity seems like something that simply happens, if we're very lucky.

In fact, we all have an inner creative side—we just need to tap into it. And while there may be some magic involved in the process, there are steps we can take to get ourselves into a place where inspiration is likely to strike. Even factors we might not associate with creativity—from sleep to our relationship with technology—can play a part.

I completely understand the sense of wonder that has led men and women through the ages to explore outer space, but I've personally always been much more fascinated with exploring inner space. There is, of course, a connection between the two. Astronauts have often reported transformational experiences when they looked back at Earth, a phenomenon that has been called the overview effect. As Edgar Mitchell, the sixth man on the moon, described it, "There was a startling recognition that the nature of the universe was not as I

had been taught . . . I not only saw the connectedness, I felt it. . . .
I was overwhelmed with the sensation of physically and mentally
extending out into the cosmos. I realized that this was a biological
response of my brain attempting to reorganize and give meaning to
information about the wonderful and awesome processes that I was
privileged to view."

   The good news is we don't need to leave Earth's atmosphere in
order to have transformational experiences. The potential is inside
us and the opportunities are all around us. And in fact, it is often the
small moments of wonder, awe, and connection that inspire us most.
All we need to do is open ourselves to these experiences and build
habits that are more likely to take us to the places—both physical
and emotional—that give us the same sense of privilege Mitchell
describes.

   Understanding the science of creativity and hearing stories from
some truly creative minds help us realize we have more power than
we think to find inspiration and tap into our inner creativity.
Whatever your idea, project, or ambition is, Microsteps will help
you bring it to life.

—*Arianna Huffington*

• • • •

THERE'S A CREATIVE pulse that beats in all of us. From the
time we're born, we have a miraculous capacity to experience
wonder and be inspired—by the world around us, by works of
art, by other people, and even by ourselves.

   But as we grow, staying connected to that creative part
of ourselves isn't so easy. The responsibilities and demands of
adulthood take over. Stressful jobs and the general busyness

of life give our days a breathless, frenetic quality. When this is the reality for so many of us, it's not surprising that creativity, inspiration, wonder, and awe might feel like relics of childhood that no longer have a place in our definition of success. We develop mindsets that prevent us from being our most creative selves.

And yet, connecting with our own creativity is essential to a thriving life. And if we're intentional about it, we can help ourselves unlock our inner creativity—not by dramatically restructuring our lives and reinventing ourselves but by taking Microsteps. We can't snap our fingers and be inspired, but we *can* create conditions that bring us closer with that part of ourselves that thrums with bold ideas, questions, and dreams.

There's no one-size-fits-all approach to unlocking our inner creativity. But sometimes all it takes is an unexpected detour—or a moment of downtime—to reframe our perspective, recharge our energy, and help us see what we hadn't seen before.

REDEFINING CREATIVITY

Somewhere between childhood and adulthood, we start to see creativity as a binary: We're either creative or we're not. Many of us allow our job to determine which camp we're in. (Graphic designer? Creative. Accountant? Not so much.) Perhaps the phrase "I don't see my job as creative so therefore I am not creative" resonates. Or maybe, with all that must be done, there just doesn't seem to be time for creativity.

But this approach to creativity is severely limiting. First of all, we are more than our jobs. And furthermore, while our work can provide meaningful opportunities for creativity, it's

THE CREATIVE ANALOGY THAT GIVES ME OPTIMISM

My nine-year-old niece, Sophie Chiaravalle, asked me to speak to her class about what exactly a producer does.

"Sure," I said, "no problem."

But it turns out it wasn't so easy. Producing isn't a profession like being a doctor, or a nurse, or a teacher. There aren't set tasks on any given day, or even set places to go. I wanted to conjure up an image so they could understand.

So I told them that a producer is someone who has a dream and tries every day to make that dream a reality.

"Imagine that dream," I said, "as a kind of huge boulder, and the producer rolling it up a ginormous mountain filled with holes, and detours, and mudslides, and often a few rattlesnakes. It's heavy, and it's hard, and it doesn't just require strength," I said. "It requires foresight, and a great deal of help from a lot of people. And even with all that help," I explained, "the producer has to think on her feet and sometimes change direction just to navigate the different obstacles and to try to reach the top. Because when she does," I told them, "she will be able to share that dream with the world."

As the image of me, I imagine, rolling some boulder was sinking in, one little boy raised his hand and said, "What happens if she doesn't make it?"

"What happens if she gets bitten by a rattlesnake, or falls into a cavern, or the boulder rolls back down the hill?"

And before I could answer, Sophie said, "She just gets up, figures a way out, and tries again."

And THAT gives me hope.

—Elaine Goldsmith-Thomas, film producer

not just a handful of traditionally creative professions that allow us to express ourselves and innovate.

We can shift our perspective and challenge the limiting beliefs we may have about what it means to be creative. These beliefs may be powerfully ingrained in us, but we have the ability to override them—with benefits to every aspect of our life.

So let's expand our understanding of creativity. Living a creative life isn't just about making things, such as painting, writing, building, or playing music. It's about awakening the almost constant state of wonder we knew as children. The triggers are there. But are we present enough to experience them? Sometimes to do this, we must look through a different set of eyes.

Instead of categorizing ourselves as creative or non-creative people, we can see that each day holds opportunities for creativity, inspiration, awe, and wonder. This reframed sense of ourselves helps us see that we have choices about what we do and how we spend our time. It separates us from a victim mentality and encourages us to make different choices that better suit our creative inclinations.

Finding that creative pulse within ourselves is all about being present in the moment. It might hit us when we're in the shower, surrounded by steam and rushing water (and finally

---

HOW I THRIVE

RICHARD BRANSON,
founder of the Virgin Group

Write down an idea right when it comes to you.

"Write it down! I can't tell you where I'd be if I hadn't had a pen on hand to write down my ideas as soon as they came to me."

• • • •

---

free of our ubiquitous devices). Or it might come to us right before we fall asleep, when we're flooded with a groggy clarity as we finally begin to think beyond our to-do list ("I hope I don't forget this burst of inspiration in the morning"). Unburdened from distractions, we may find our thoughts wander to strange, beautiful places. Why not give ourselves permission to linger for a while?

Finally, we must free ourselves of the notion of the *bigness* of living a life of creativity, inspiration, and wonder. Our sense of wonder is often stronger when it's provoked by things that are ordinary and unassuming—our children's faces, a flower, a thunderstorm. As Walt Whitman said, "After all, the great lesson is that no special natural sights—not Alps, Niagara, Yosemite or anything else—is more grand or more beautiful than the ordinary sunrise and sunset, earth and sky, the common trees and grass."

HOW I THRIVE

TONI KO, founder of NYX Cosmetics

When you hit a mental block, go to sleep. You will wake up refreshed and able to think clearer.

"This is about giving your brain a break from being fatigued. Just like how your body can't perform its best when your body is fatigued, your brain can't function at its highest capacity when you're mentally fatigued."

• • •

SCREENING IN WONDER

Peace and silence are increasingly hard to find. If we are living in a frenetic swirl of activity, it's much, much harder to try to create something beautiful, think through a problem, or appreciate a scene of natural beauty. How can we achieve clarity when we're tethered to our buzzing, chirping phones? How can our next idea blossom if our jobs carry us from one meeting to the next without any pause to recharge? We are wired, plugged in, constantly catered to, and increasingly terrified of silence, unaware of what it has to offer. We drown out the big but simple questions of life with the simplistic sound bites of our 500-channel-and-nothing-on universe.

So as we try to get past the static, we can start by setting boundaries with our technology. While it's true that our devices can stoke our creativity and help us experience wonder, too much time with screens has a way of dulling our creative faculties—and sapping our attention so that we miss the kind of everyday wonders Walt Whitman rightly celebrated. If you've ever found yourself photographing experiences before you've actually experienced them, you know how it is.

Sherry Turkle, MIT professor and author of *Alone Together*, has written about the cost of constantly documenting—that is, photographing—our lives. These interruptions, she writes, "make it hard to settle into serious conversations with ourselves and with other people because emotionally, we keep ourselves available to be taken away from everything." And by obsessively documenting our experiences, we never truly have them.

BOREDOM IS OUR FRIEND

We may associate success with busyness and being always "on," but research shows that the empty moments in our day, when our minds can disconnect and wander freely, boost creativity.

Albert Einstein recognized the benefits of ennui long before there was science to prove it. He famously spent the year after his high school graduation "aimlessly loafing," thinking outside the stifling walls of academia and mulling the ideas that would radically transform our understanding of the world.

Bill Gates has his biannual Think Week, a seven-day retreat where he hides away in his cabin in the Pacific Northwest, with no company except his own thoughts and a pile of thought proposals. While we can't all take a week away from our lives to hide out in a secluded thinking cabin, the ritual that Gates has adopted tells us a lot about the necessity of slowing down and taking time for ourselves. Whether you're in need of a few additional vacation days, a weekend without screen time, or just a few moments of mindful meditation before bed, taking time to unplug and recharge is critical for our mental, physical, and psychological well-being—and fostering our creativity is a big part of that.

"The capacity to be bored is so important because it is tied to the capacity to look within to an enlivened and enlivening self," Sherry Turkle told Thrive. "Boredom is an essential part of our creativity and emotional development."

And yet, when faced with nothing to do, we compulsively seek out distraction. In the absence of productivity, we feel unworthy; we misinterpret *doing* nothing for *being* nothing. Our aversion to ennui is nothing new: in 1930, the British philosopher Bertrand Russell wrote that "we are less bored than our ancestors were, but we are more afraid of boredom."

Given our propensity to avoid it, scheduling time for boredom is a helpful way to prioritize it each day. We can go for a device-free stroll. We can sit still with our eyes closed. We can allow ourselves to daydream, which is not only a sign of higher intelligence, as studies suggest, but can also be deeply pleasurable. Any one of these can be practiced in brief increments each day. While boredom can feel uncomfortable at first, we'll be more likely to find answers and connect with our creativity and sense of wonder if we sit with the feeling and remain unplugged.

SPARKING YOUR NEXT EUREKA MOMENT

Inspiration doesn't always come in flashes of lightning. In fact, with Microsteps, we can move from passively waiting to actively creating conditions where our best ideas are more likely to strike.

Often, this begins with stepping off the treadmill of constant connectivity and busyness—even for a little while. If we're stressed and burned out, buried in to-do lists and email inboxes, then we simply can't get ourselves to a place of creativity. Be aware, we may face some internal resistance here—after all, we've been conditioned to prize an always "on" way of working and living and to view downtime as the enemy of productivity. But when we begin to create conditions that allow us more breathing room—physically, mentally, and spiritually—our world opens up. We become open to possibilities we didn't see before. And we grant ourselves access to the parts of life—and parts of ourselves—where our best ideas can be found.

Eve Rodsky, author of *Fair Play*, calls it unicorn space: the precious time and space to explore your creativity and be uniquely you. We've come to view this time as a luxury—something we enjoyed as children, but that doesn't fit into our overstuffed, responsible adult lives. But according to Rodsky, unicorn space is essential to our overall happiness—and also to our ability to be the best version of ourselves for the people who matter most in our lives.

So how do we find our unicorn space? Rodsky is clear. "It doesn't exist until you create it. You need to carve it out for yourself."

And Microsteps can help. Even if you start with only five minutes a week, set time on your calendar to focus on your passions each week, even for just a few minutes. Play guitar, paint, write poetry, look at the stars—whatever it is that fills you up with joy and purpose. You might feel at first like you're being bad—taking a few minutes for yourself, the horror!—but over time, by showing you're serious about your passions by going beyond the idea and taking actionable steps toward them, you'll see that allowing yourself this time is much more than a mere indulgence.

If you're hooked on the idea of unicorn space and looking for new ideas, there's no shortage of ways to spark your inner creativity and draw you out of your comfort zone in ways that might surprise you.

Taking time each day to journal or freewrite can help us sort through mental clutter and harness our creativity. In *The Artist's Way*, a creativity bible that has sold more than four million copies since it was published in 1992, author Julia Cameron recommends writing three full pages by hand before doing anything else in the morning.

Reading a work of fiction can also spark creativity, as short stories and novels have a way of inciting our imagination. When so much of our work requires us to seek cognitive closure—conclusions, takeaways, absolutes—reading fiction takes us down more open-ended paths, encouraging us to see possibilities in our lives we may have otherwise missed.

We can also be more hands on with our approach. Mixing oil paints on a canvas, or swapping one ingredient for another in a recipe, can be a creative playground. If you have children, plop beside them while they play and take part. Putter with beads, fill in a coloring book. These activities reunite us with our inner child—and help us recharge in the midst of stressful days.

Some creative crafts, like knitting, quilting, or needlework, are linked to psychological benefits. A survey of over 3,500 knitters found the activity to be linked with stress relief and improved communication with others, and other studies reinforce the connection between creative craft hobbies and enhanced well-being. Crafting combines self-expression and problem-solving in a low-stakes environment, creating a sensation akin to meditation.

"Ideas are like fish," wrote director and longtime meditator David Lynch. "If you want to catch little fish, you can stay in the shallow water. But if you want to catch the big fish, you've got to go deeper. Down deep, the fish are more powerful and more pure. They're huge and abstract. And they're very beautiful." (And yes, the title of his book is *Catching the Big Fish*.)

Priming our physical environment for creativity can also be helpful in boosting it. One study found that working in darkness or dim lighting can loosen our minds and encourage an abundant outpouring of ideas. We can also prime ourselves for creativity by knowing what distractions and obstacles to remove from our environment. Many accomplished writers, including Jonathan Franzen and Zadie Smith, swear by working in places without an internet connection. Few of us are immune to the temptations (and time-wasters) of the internet and social media, so we can help ourselves by banishing them temporarily in order to plumb the depths of our ideas, as David Lynch describes.

To start building creative routines into your day, try scheduling short bursts of creative work time on your calendar. No amount of time is too small. How you spend these minutes is entirely up to you: freewriting, walking, playing piano, whatever works. Keep at it and you'll begin to build the habit of prioritizing creativity.

HOW SLEEP MAKES US MORE CREATIVE

As science overwhelmingly demonstrates, sleep plays a vital role in our decision-making, emotional intelligence, and cognitive function. It's a vessel for our big ideas.

That's why the Microsteps for improving sleep shared in Chapter 1 aren't just an investment in your well-being, they're like kindling for creativity. In addition to processing and strengthening short- and long-term memory, sleep can transform them in a process linked to creativity, according to a Brazilian study, which found that during REM sleep neural processes not only strengthen connections between neurons but also reorganize them. We see this connection most prominently in the world of art, especially with dreams, which author and journalist Arthur Koestler described as "periods of incubation" that redirect our attention to "something not previously noted." The list of great works inspired by dreams is as long as it is dazzling. "Let It Be" came to Paul McCartney in a dream he had about his mother during the time the Beatles were breaking up. Many of Salvador Dalí's surrealist paintings were the products of dreams; he described them as "hand-painted dream photographs."

In the realm of science and innovation, breakthroughs ranging from the periodic table of elements to Google can be credited to dreams.

Sleep-sparked breakthroughs are accessible not just to artists and inventors but to all of us. The self-doubts that limit us during the day are quieted during sleep, and our creativity

---

HOW I THRIVE

MARIE FORLEO,
entrepreneur and author

Each morning, make time to prioritize movement.

"If I'm working on a new writing project or something highly creative, journaling happens and then some type of movement. Whether that's a little bit of dance or working out, using an app on my phone to get in a quick seven-minute workout or walking around the block—even a little movement really gets me going."

• • • •

can find expression without judgment. Dr. J. Allan Hobson, a Harvard Medical School psychiatrist, summed it up this way: "Dreaming may be our most creative conscious state, one in which the chaotic, spontaneous recombination of cognitive elements produces novel configurations of information: new ideas."

Through Microsteps, we can prime our brains for novel configurations, whether we're aiming to change the world with our next big idea or simply looking to enhance the quality of daily life. Journaling about our dreams is a simple way to use them to our creative advantage, according to 2016 research published in the journal *Consciousness and Cognition*. And a 2019 study published in the *Journal of Creative Behavior* found that greater dream recall was linked with greater creativity because of the way it encourages our dreaming minds to interact with our waking ones.

By taking just a few minutes to jot down our dreams, we can transport ourselves out of the logical, linear realm in which we spend so much of our time and expand into a place with different challenges and rewards.

As dreams researcher Kelly Bulkeley writes in *Psychology Today*, "Take your time when initially recording a dream, and

---

HOW I THRIVE

JULIE LARSON-GREEN, chief experience officer at Qualtrics

Brainstorm with a group of people to cultivate creativity.

"I get my energy from being around other people. When I'm working, I get energized when I'm problem-solving and brainstorming with a group of people. I love bouncing ideas off different people."

• • • •

don't worry if some aspects of the dream are vague, fragmentary, or impossible to describe. Just write them out as best as you can. All of these fragments can be sources of unexpected significance when you look at the dreams over time."

FINDING CREATIVITY AT WORK

In 2018, research from LinkedIn Learning found that creativity is the skill companies are looking for most. "If you want to 'future-proof' your career, there's no better approach than focusing on thinking more creatively. Stop settling for solutions that worked previously and push yourself to think of newer, better ideas," Paul Petrone, the head of Academic and Government Marketing at LinkedIn Learning, wrote.

Indeed, creative thinking is an invaluable part of our work, whether we're a well-established CEO or we're just getting started in our career. But when deliverables and deadlines are at stake, the charge to be creative can be stressful—and that's where Microsteps come in.

Changing scenery and going for a brief walk can do the trick. We know the benefits of walking to physical and mental health; it turns out walking is shown to increase creativity by as much as 60 percent. Ernest Hemingway said that walking was a tool to develop his best thoughts while mulling a problem. "I would walk along the quais when I had finished work or when I was trying to think something out," he wrote in *A Moveable Feast*. "It was easier to think if I was walking and doing something or seeing people doing something that they understood." Friedrich Nietzsche went even further and proclaimed that "only thoughts conceived while walking have any value."

Walking isn't only a way to respond to a mental rut; it can be a way to prevent one from happening. Try swapping your next sit-down brainstorming session, or another meeting that requires innovative thinking, with a walking meeting. You'll be less likely to look at your devices, and the movement and outdoor stimuli will get the creative juices flowing.

Unlocking creativity at work also means knowing when it's time to call it a day. At Thrive Global, we believe so strongly in this principle that we've made it one of our cultural values: "We relentlessly prioritize and are comfortable with incompletions." The more interesting, ambitious, creative, and meaningful we want our work to be, the more we'll need to not only be comfortable with incompletions but embrace them. And when we can do this each day, we'll arrive the next day recharged and ready to tackle challenges, seize opportunities, and create new possibilities.

And it's not just about work. Knowing when to declare an end to the day allows us to take valuable time for ourselves, whether it's our unicorn space or unstructured time to do nothing at all. Spending time this way may seem unproductive or even wasteful, but it's actually essential for helping us recharge and connect to ourselves in deeply meaningful ways.

WONDER IS A PRECONDITION FOR LIFE

Wonder is at the heart of creativity. Einstein wrote that whoever lacks the capacity to wonder, "whoever cannot contemplate or know the deep shudder of the soul in enchantment, might just as well be dead for he has already closed his eyes upon life."

He was onto something, as studies show that wonder and awe can improve our well-being.

Research published in the journal *Psychological Science* found that "experiences of awe bring people into the present moment, and being in the present moment underlies awe's capacity to adjust time perception, influence decisions, and make life feel more satisfying than it would otherwise."

So how do we tap into this feeling on a regular basis? Traveling is a wonderful mechanism, but a vacation isn't always feasible, nor is it enough to nourish our ongoing need for wonder and awe.

Instead, we can cultivate wonder with Microsteps, and regularly set out—for however short a time—on a journey inward. Spending a few minutes outdoors each day, disconnected from work and our devices, is a great way to begin. When we're in nature, it's easier for us to feel transcendent and connected to something larger than ourselves, experts say. Don't worry if you live in a place where nature in the form of canyons, wide open landscapes, and vast bodies of water isn't readily available. We can cultivate a similar effect by moving slowly through

---

HOW I THRIVE

JERRY SALTZ, *New York Magazine*'s Pulitzer Prize–winning art critic

Embrace failure as part of the creative process.

"Never, ever think about creating something good. Good is boring. Ninety-five percent of what I write is crapola and I just cut it to find the 5 percent that might be worth putting out into the world. You have to open up and pursue that kind of radical vulnerability."

---

whatever outdoors are closest to us, or even by just looking up—whether it's day or night, cloudy or star-packed, the sky can often inspire awe.

Listening to music is another great conduit, as research shows it's a common trigger of awe. There's also visual art. Museums and galleries remain among the few oases that can deliver what has become increasingly rare in our world: the opportunity to disconnect from our hyperconnected lives and experience the feeling of wonder.

And then, sometimes the best way to experience awe is to simply look around at the people closest to us and pause long enough to appreciate something about them. In studies, this is referred to as interpersonal awe, which is "defined by themes of virtue or excellence of character."

Take a moment today and think of a precious person in your life. How did the world bring you together? Awe can be found where we don't necessarily expect it, in the people we meet and the experiences we have. These small wonders are indeed something to feel grateful for.

MICROSTEP DIARY

Mallory Stratton, senior product content editor

MICROSTEP: Declare an end to the day, even if you haven't completed everything.

Why I Chose It

I have a hard time leaving work with items still left on my to-do list; I'd rather just chug through, even if it keeps me there until 9 p.m. or later. My goal was to establish a habit of calling it a night by 7 p.m., emergencies notwithstanding.

What Happened

I spent my first week of the challenge at the office long past 7 p.m., so I nudged my benchmark back to a more realistic time. Once I did that, I started seeing real results. I wrapped up before 7:30 p.m. almost every night. I was surprised at how well I was sticking to it. It had become an external rule, a structural reality.

For the first time in my career, I truly feel the connection between my energy levels and my creative output. I've become more attuned to when I'm on my A-game and when I'm running on reserves. Instead of hitting a wall and trying to push through it, I learned to set my to-dos aside for a fresh look in the morning; staying late wasn't going to make ideas or solutions materialize any faster.

I'm not perfect, but packing up by 7:30 p.m. has become implicit enough that I now do it without a second thought. But what's struck me the most was how with all this newfound freedom, I didn't really know what to do with myself. I never realized just how deeply I've been undervaluing my time.

MICROSTEPS

Schedule time to go outside. Just a few minutes during the day can make a big difference. Simply being outdoors and surrounded by nature not only improves your well-being but inspires you to be a more creative, more present version of yourself.

Take short pauses throughout the day. After a period of intense focus, or when you're feeling stuck, taking just a few minutes away from your desk and screens can help free you from the demands of your inbox and your to-do list.

Take a planned detour. Travel is a great way to take you out of your comfort zone, but you don't need to go around the world or even leave town to stimulate your mind in creative ways. Find an everyday opportunity, like turning down an unfamiliar side street, to expose yourself to new people, sights, and sensations.

Add a short story or novel to your reading list. So much of our work requires us to seek cognitive closure—conclusions, takeaways, absolutes—but reading fiction boosts creativity by taking us down more open-ended paths.

Plan a visit to your local museum or art gallery. These places remain among the few oases that can deliver what has become increasingly rare in our world: the opportunity to disconnect from our hyperconnected lives and experience the feeling of wonder.

Make at least one meeting each day device-free. You'll be more focused, engaged, and productive, and your team will be more creative without distractions from phones and computers.

Declare an end to the day, even if you haven't completed everything. Truly prioritizing means being comfortable with incompletions. When you take time to recharge, you'll return ready to seize opportunities.

Let yourself be bored. The next time you're waiting in line, stuck in traffic, or someone is late for a meeting, embrace it instead of immediately going to your phone or tablet. Unstructured moments can lead to inspiration, creativity, reflection, and connection.

Take a moment to look up next time you step outside. Every day, allow yourself to take in the wonders around you: the sky, the stars, mountains, clouds. Taking time to appreciate beauty, vastness, and mystery has benefits that last long after you've stopped looking up!

Read the biography of someone you admire. Reading stories of people you admire isn't just a way to find inspiration—you can actually learn from and emulate their methods of building self-awareness in the course of their lives.

HOW YOU CAN THRIVE

Think about the times in your life when you've been the most creative—what helped inspire that creativity in you?

When was the last time you made time for an activity you're passionate about that brings you joy?

What are some limiting beliefs you have around creativity? For example, *I'm not a creative person* or *There's not much in my life to inspire me.*

Did any of the science or stories in this chapter help you think differently about the nature of creativity or how we can tap into our sense of wonder in everyday ways?

What's one Microstep you can implement today to spark your inner creativity?

8

PURPOSE AND MEANING

*W*e all want lives of purpose and meaning. I believe it's one of our fundamental instincts in life—that drive for self-discovery, self-knowledge, and to feel like we're part of something larger than ourselves. It's what connects us all.

But, as the renowned Vietnamese Buddhist monk Thich Nhat Hanh put it, "It has never been easier to run away from ourselves." It's not hard to feel so overwhelmed by the next items on our ever-growing to-do lists that we fail to look up and nurture that sense of meaning and purpose that we all share. While the world bombards us with insistent, flashing, buzzing, and vibrating appeals to keep our heads down and just get through the day, there are few worldly signals reminding us to connect with the essence of who we are. So that's up to us. And when we do feed our sense of meaning and purpose, we expand our boundaries. Our possibilities expand rather than contract.

In one survey, nine out of ten career professionals said they'd accept lower future earnings for work that was more meaningful. But meaning can be found in any job and in any activity. Instead of focusing on what we do, we can instead consider questions like: Who benefits from what we do? Who do we connect with? What impact *are we having on those around us? When we connect with our sense of purpose, we find greater connection and, in turn, greater purpose.*

If there were a theory of everything in the study of our emotional universe, empathy and giving would be at the center of it. Modern science has overwhelmingly confirmed the wisdom of early philosophers and religious traditions. Empathy, compassion, and giving—which is simply empathy and compassion in action—are the molecular building blocks of our being. With them we expand and thrive; without them we wither.

One of my favorite quotes is from the thirteenth-century Persian poet Rumi: you should "live life as if everything is rigged in your favor." We can't know what's in store for us, but we can choose to find meaning and purpose and possibility in our daily lives. And when we do, we'll truly thrive.

—Arianna Huffington

● ● ● ●

"WHAT IS A good life?" has been a question asked by philosophers going back in time to the ancient Greeks. But somewhere along the line we abandoned the question and shifted our attention to other matters: how much money we can make, how big a house we can buy, and how high we can climb up the career ladder. Those are legitimate concerns, but they are far from the only ones that matter for creating a successful life.

So far, we've seen how Microsteps can transform our physical and mental well-being, improve our performance, and enhance our connections with others. Now, we'll explore a theme that in many ways encapsulates them all.

If we are really going to live a good life, we need to dig deeper—to find out what makes us tick as human beings, what makes our lives meaningful, what brings us joy. These may seem like big, lofty questions, but exploring them doesn't need to be daunting. By taking Microsteps, we can shift our perspective, open ourselves up to possibilities we may have missed, and tap into something larger than ourselves.

GRATITUDE CAN CHANGE YOUR LIFE

In 1994, twenty-five years after his historic moon landing, Neil Armstrong did something we don't often associate with people who have achieved groundbreaking accomplishments. He wrote a thank you note. He sent it to the individuals who helped to make it possible for him to walk on the moon. Specifically, he thanked the engineers who created his spacecraft for its toughness and reliability. Armstrong wrote, "To all of you who made it all that it was, I send a quarter century's worth of thanks and congratulations."

Thank you: two simple words with profound power. Generous and moving, they demonstrate that Armstrong understood the value of appreciation and teamwork. Thanking everyone who supported him in that historic endeavor was meaningful for him and no doubt for all those who received his letter. It was a recognition that they were all connected, and it is a reminder to us that all lives are purposeful.

Saying thank you often and sincerely, expressing heartfelt appreciation both to others and even to yourself, can add purpose and meaning to everything you do. The ancients certainly

GIVING CAN TRANSFORM YOU

Time is our greatest resource. A finite resource. All of us are living off of a carefully constructed time budget, rightfully so. Donating time is hence one of the most generous forms of giving, and the more we give, the more time-affluent we feel. The greatest beneficiary of giving is, perhaps, oneself as there is renewed sense of hope and energy, leaving us feeling fulfilled.

There's evidence to prove that gratitude is the highest form of thought and the healthiest of all human emotions. The will to pay forward is, therefore, amongst the purest of intentions, I believe. As the saying goes, gratitude is happiness doubled by wonder.

—Vinutha Narayan, global manager, Strategic Projects at Google

knew the value of giving thanks. Cicero wrote that "gratitude is not only the greatest of virtues but the parent of all the others." It took a few thousand years, but those words of wisdom have since been validated by a mountain of science.

It's no coincidence that gratitude, along with other structural supports of our well-being, has been at the core of every tradition that focuses on what it means to live a good life. The Stoics saw gratitude as a kind of medicine; saying thank you for every experience was the key to mental health. "Convince yourself that everything is the gift of the gods," was how Marcus Aurelius put it, "that things are good and always will be."

Adopting such an attitude may seem impossible or even inappropriate when so many of the things we see or experience are *not* good, when crises and injustices threaten to plunge us into pessimism. But feeling gratitude is not the same as putting on blinders or denying the need for change. It is a way of acknowledging that while we cannot control all our circumstances, we can control our responses. Far from being a weak response, gratitude strengthens our defenses against outside forces that seek to diminish us.

Say thanks to a rude person. Say thanks to a bungled project. Why? Because it may have just saved you from something far worse, but also because you have essentially no choice in the matter. Epictetus said that every situation has two handles. Which are you going to decide to hold on to? The anger or the appreciation? The one of resentment or of thanks?

We're taught from a young age to write those notes and to say "thank you." But as we get older, expressions of gratitude can become reflexes or afterthoughts. We may think it doesn't really matter, or it may not even occur to us in the course of our fast-moving days.

But saying thank you has a direct impact on our physical and mental health. One study from Indiana University found that practicing gratitude alters brain function in people with depression. Neuroplasticity (our brain's ability to constantly create new neural pathways) gives us the power to train our brains to seek out moments of gratitude. That's good news for those who are concerned that they are naturally negative and might be stuck in a glass-half-empty mentality forever. With conscious practice, you have the ability to rewire your brain.

Dr. Martin Seligman, one of the founders of the field of positive psychology, has shown that the benefits of a single gratitude exercise—writing and delivering a thank you letter—can last for an entire month.

Gratitude works its magic by serving as an antidote to negative emotions, protecting us from cynicism, entitlement, anger, and resignation. It activates regions of the brain associated with pleasure, reward, and stress relief. It sounds obvious that being grateful is positive, but it goes much deeper. Appreciation for the blessings in our life helps us stay present. Rather than incessantly wishing we were richer, more successful, more attractive, and happier, by focusing on what's good in our lives right now, we automatically feel better.

HOW I THRIVE

TIFFANY SHLAIN, filmmaker and author

As soon as you wake up, write down three things you're grateful for.

"It's a simple morning practice that keeps the world from coming at me before I have fully woken up. What a profoundly different way to frame the day."

● ● ● ●

That doesn't mean abandoning goals and dreams. In fact, if we accept where we are, with appreciation for everything that's good in our lives, we may find ourselves in a better position to actually go out and achieve those dreams.

It doesn't take a lot of effort to incorporate more gratitude into our lives. Oxford clinical psychologist Mark Williams describes gratitude as "intentionally bringing into awareness the tiny, previously unnoticed elements of the day." One suggestion: Write down a list of what you're grateful for before you go to bed. It will lower your stress levels and give you a greater sense of calm at night.

In addition to being grateful to our families and friends, it is also important to express our gratitude at work. Giving authentic positive feedback is often overlooked though. Researchers at the John Templeton Foundation found that nearly half of us will say thank you on a regular basis to someone we're immediately related to, but only 15 percent of us will say thank you at work. So we need to shift our mindset around gratitude.

Try practicing this Microstep: Take a moment each day to compliment a coworker on a job well done. You have an immediate opportunity to add something meaningful to someone else's day. And you might be surprised what an impact you can have. It's a practice LEMS sneakers entrepreneur Andrew Rademacher does every day. "When everyone leaves the office for the day, I tell each person thanks, and express my gratitude to them," says Rademacher, who set out to create a new work culture when he founded his company in 2008. "I also continue to tell my wife thank you for everything she does to help us in life," he says.

The benefits of gratitude are countless. It can lower levels of stress and depression, and improve sleep. In adolescents, gratitude has been found to reduce materialism and increase generosity, and even lead to healthier eating. At the other end of life, gratitude has been found to reduce loneliness in the elderly. As Charles Dickens wrote, "reflect upon your present blessings, of which every man has plenty; not on your past misfortunes, of which all men have some."

And it's not just our present blessings. The power of gratitude can also extend to what *hasn't* happened—all those close shaves with "disaster" of some kind or another, all the bad things that could happen to us and just . . . don't. That distance between them happening and not happening is grace. The power of being grateful for our lives right now is summed up in this life-affirming quote (attributed to the eighth-century Muslim jurist Imam Al-Shafi'i): "My heart is at ease knowing that what was meant for me will never miss me, and that what misses me was never meant for me."

WORK THAT MEANS SOMETHING

There's a famous story about President John F. Kennedy's visit to the NASA space center in 1962. During his tour, JFK noticed a janitor carrying a broom. He walked over to the man and said, "Hi, I'm Jack Kennedy. What are you doing?" "Well, Mr. President," the janitor responded, "I'm helping put a man on the moon."

To casual observers a NASA janitor was just cleaning the building. But in the larger story unfolding around him, he was helping to make history. He was able to connect his individual contribution to something much larger than himself. Most of us could learn a thing or two from that janitor. You can do the same thing yourself and connect your individual contribution to something greater. After completing a project, write an email thanking a colleague (or your whole team) for their support. The simple act of putting your gratitude in writing will strengthen your relationships with coworkers and allow you to reflect on how much their support helped you before you move on to the next task.

We tend to overlook the meaning and impact of what we have created—including at work. According to Thrive Global's chief training officer Joey Hubbard, it's worth asking these questions in relation to the work you do: What do you create? Who do you create it for? And why?

We also tend to underestimate the meaning we bring to our own lives, the lives of others, and even to the broader community. That's because we often have a limiting paradigm about our value and worth. Hubbard has worked with call center workers around the world and asks them these three questions. Often, they respond: "I don't create anything." Or "I answer angry phone calls all day. I just do it to make a living." But in fact, a call center worker is on the front lines of the customer experience. They're dealing with real people every day. And because they have an opportunity to make or break a person's experience, they're key brand ambassadors. Whatever work we do, when we shift the paradigm,

---

HOW I THRIVE

KARENA DAWN, author, cofounder of Tone It Up

Make a "happy list" of all the things in your life that bring you joy, and look at it when you're feeling down.

"I like to make a 'happy list' of the things that bring me joy, like meditation, exercise, being outdoors, music, and spending time with my loved ones and my pets. This is an amazing solution for everyone! Keep this list in your phone or in a journal on your bedside table. Anytime you're feeling anxious or overwhelmed, you can always look at it as a reminder of what makes you happiest."

---

we can discover a lot more meaning than what's visible on the surface.

As Hubbard advises, one of the best ways to connect with that deeper purpose or meaning is by a simple reframing. Instead of focusing on what you do, consider who benefits. When you're struggling with your work, think of a person or population who might benefit from it. It just takes a thought, and you'll be better equipped to move through momentary stress (or other concerns) and see the true value of what you're doing. Plus, finding meaning in what you are doing will ignite your creativity.

There's plenty of evidence to support the idea of finding value in your work. In a well-known study, Yale School of Management professor Amy Wrzesniewski interviewed hospital workers and discovered that they found their work highly meaningful and fulfilling. Of course, that may not sound surprising, since hospitals are filled with doctors and nurses who save lives and care for people. But Wrzesniewski didn't interview doctors and nurses; she interviewed custodial workers. Here's a quote from a study participant:

"I have so much to offer sick people. Because when I don't feel good or when I have had to have surgeries, the one thing that has gotten me through has been . . . jokes, just being pleasant, being upbeat, and having a great attitude. And that's what I enjoy most about being here."

These custodial workers found their work deeply meaningful. They were able to forge bonds with patients and see who benefited from their work.

We all need to feel valued, and that our work matters. In fact, a desire for more meaning and purpose is one of the overarching

THE FOOTPRINTS WE LEAVE BEHIND

Purpose need not be anything grand. It can be a small act of kindness, done over a long period of time, with great love. As long as we are doing what is useful to others, as long as we make a difference to at least one person, we will be happy, and life will be purposeful. As Emerson said, "The purpose of life is not to be happy. It is to be useful, to be honorable, to be compassionate, to have it make some difference that you have lived and lived well."

Purpose is about going beyond yourself. Finding your purpose essentially boils down to finding those one or two things that are bigger than yourself, and bigger than those around you. Ask the question: What is your legacy? What are people going to say about you when you are gone? Imagine a world without yourself and the footprints you want to leave behind!

—V. R. Ferose, senior vice president
and head of SAP Engineering Academy

trends of the modern workplace. According to a 2017 survey of over 2,000 workers by BetterUp, a San Francisco–based leadership development platform, nine out of ten career professionals told researchers that they would sacrifice 23 percent of their future earnings for "work that is always meaningful."

And when you're able to connect to that sense of purpose, your performance gets a boost. How do we tap into that sense of purpose? Here's one easy suggestion: Tell a nonwork friend or family member about a project you're excited about. Their comments and questions may help you see meaning where you didn't before, and that in turn may boost your performance and open up a whole new world of possibilities.

And, by the way, whatever work you are currently engaged in, you can always set an intention to look for work in a field that you are passionate about. It's perfectly possible to do both, bring value to the job you are doing and pursue a "dream career" at the same time. On the space theme once more, NASA cadet Alyssa Carson has realized her own dream at an incredibly young age—she is nineteen years old—and she suggests this Microstep: Go out of your way to discuss your aspirations with coworkers and strangers; talk about your dreams to everyone, because you never know where an opportunity might be. As the world's youngest astronaut-in-training, Carson has another big dream: she wants to be the first human to set foot on Mars.

Often, connecting to a sense of purpose is about knowing where to look. As Jen Fisher, chief well-being officer at Deloitte points out, it is a misconception that purpose is this "huge, elusive thing. In reality, discovering purpose is rarely

---

HOW I THRIVE

ANTONI POROWSKI, food and wine connoisseur, Queer Eye, and restaurateur

Each day, say no to one thing that doesn't serve you.

"When I was saying yes to everything, to every job opportunity that came my way, I spread myself too thin. I realized I wasn't performing well at work events, and wasn't having any downtime or just plain fun with friends."

• • • •

an earth-shattering, lightbulb moment—or something you find all at once." That's where Microsteps come in. Little by little, we can move closer to the kind of meaningful life we want.

THE SURPRISING REWARDS
WE GET FROM GIVING

We know it's important to give back and contribute to our community. But the power of giving goes much deeper. Going beyond ourselves and stepping out of our comfort zones to serve others is one of the most effective ways to boost our well-being, transforming the giver as much as the recipients. When we give, we feel good physically and we grow spiritually. Giving works because it helps us to gain perspective and connect with our true, compassionate nature. It jump-starts our transition from a go-getter to a go-giver, and reconnects us to the world and to the natural abundance in our own lives.

Sometimes, with so much focus on materialism in our society, it seems that the whole world shrinks down to just ourselves—and when that happens, the smallest problems or reversals of fortunes can throw us. Our entire narrative revolves around ourselves. But when we include others and widen the circle of our concern, we're less concerned with the self—and it is much easier to gain empathy, to find gratitude, and to connect with our better selves.

There are countless stories about the commendable grand scale philanthropy and volunteering that people in the public eye do all the time. For example, musician and activist Lenny Kravitz's passion project is an effort to help the underserved residents in the Bahamas, where he spent summers as a child, get access to dental care. And former First Lady Michelle Obama has used her voice to speak out about so many causes that are close to her heart, from her Let's Move initiative to her partnership work with nonprofit Be the Change to her push to grant education access to girls worldwide through the Girls Opportunity Alliance.

But giving is just as valuable on a very small scale. For example, getting groceries for an older person in your community, or spending an hour with someone who lives alone and would welcome the company. You could use a skill or talent you have to help someone who could benefit from it, which could be anything from helping with home repairs to accounting to cooking a meal for someone.

Giving will reconnect you to the world and to the natural abundance in your own life. Consider making small gestures of kindness and giving a habit, and pay attention to how this affects your mind, your emotions, and your body.

Sometimes though, the idea of giving even an hour of our time might seem overwhelming. Where is the time to give when we are busily engrossed in our own lives, raising our children, working, doing household chores, and paying bills? What's fascinating though is that when we *do* make the time to volunteer, time has a way of expanding.

A fascinating study from the Wharton, Yale, and Harvard business schools compared three groups of participants: one that wasted time, one that spent time on themselves, and one that gave their time away doing something for someone else. As it turned out, the third group had significantly higher feelings of "time affluence"—by giving their time away, they literally felt like they had created more time in their lives.

And, even more fascinating, because of the boosted feelings of self-efficacy that helping others had given them, they were also more likely to commit to additional future engagements, even though they were very busy. And it makes sense. Giving answers our fundamental need for human connection. As Mia Birdsong puts it in *How We Show Up*, "The thing is, we love to help. Our best self gets a positive feeling from supporting others. It's a feeling that is not about the gratitude we receive or the points we earn, but an alignment with love and care that fills us. When we see someone experience relief or ease or happiness because we helped them, we are filled. It also reminds us that we are not out here alone, we don't achieve or thrive, or survive or get by, on our own."

> HOW I THRIVE
>
> **MARIA MENOUNOS**, TV host and entrepreneur
>
> **Take a few deep breaths when you wake up.**
>
> "I'll go out to my front yard and take some deep breaths, and just look at the trees and the grass, and be grateful for that moment."
>
> • • • •

Giving is quite simply transformational. It helps us tap into our purpose, and as any regular volunteer will testify, it brings us an immeasurable sense of joy too. There's a reason why in practically every religious and spiritual tradition, giving of oneself is a key step on the path to fulfillment. "A generous person will prosper; whoever refreshes others will be refreshed," reads Proverbs. "Through selfless service, you will always be fruitful and find the fulfillment of your desires," says Sri Krishna in the Bhagavad Gita.

Philosophers have long known that our well-being is deeply connected to our compassion and giving. In the Bible's Book of Acts, Jesus says that "There is more happiness in giving than there is in receiving"; in 63 AD Seneca wrote, "No one can live happily who has regard for himself alone and transforms everything into a question of his own utility."

Or, as a more modern-day sage, David Letterman, put it in 2013: "I have found that the only thing that does bring you happiness is doing something good for somebody who is incapable of doing it for themselves."

Jillian Michaels, the fitness guru and television personality, says volunteering regularly has a profound impact on her life. "I've been working a lot with the United Nations Refugee Agency, and it helps me feel less helpless when I'm involved and I'm taking steps to try to make the world a tiny bit better."

Science has validated the idea of giving again and again. One study found that volunteering at least once a week gives you the same boost to well-being as a salary increase from $20,000 to $75,000. A Harvard Business School study showed that "donating to charity has a similar relationship to subjective well-being as a doubling of household income." The same study found that students who were told to spend a small amount of money on someone else were happier than students who were told to spend it on themselves.

The positive effect doesn't just come from the idea of donating some money—it comes from the connection enabled by the giving. In this study, researchers from Simon Fraser University, the University of British Columbia, and Harvard Business School gave participants $10 gift cards. One group was instructed to spend it on themselves. Another was instructed to give it to someone else to spend at Starbucks, but not go with them. And the third was told to give it to someone else and go with them to Starbucks to spend it. The result? In the words of the authors, "Participants who spent on others in a way that allowed for social connection experienced the highest levels of happiness at the end of the day."

It's exactly how changing a habit works—by being willing to take a first step, believing in the possibility that we can be someone better, then following our aspiration and continuing to take small steps. We build up our moral muscle by exercising it. Without the authority of this moral instinct to improve ourselves, our ethical sense becomes nothing more than a fear that there may be something or someone watching.

People are often motivated to give in times of crisis—like the COVID-19 pandemic when so many suffered, lost loved ones, and lost their jobs. We also see it in very obvious ways in the collective response to natural disasters. But we don't need extreme events or natural disasters to spur us to tap into our natural humanity. After all, we know there are people in need all the time, in every city, in every community.

It's about doing whatever we can to widen the circle of our concern. It's not just good for the world, it's good for us. And all we need to do is just widen our definition of self-care. Because creating a healthy self-care routine includes making time to care for others. Or as Eleanor Roosevelt put it: "Since you get more joy out of giving joy to others, you should put a good deal of thought into the happiness that you are able to give."

LOOKING INSIDE OURSELVES

To connect with a larger sense of purpose, we must first connect with ourselves. Establishing and maintaining this connection is anything but easy when we're up against the stresses and demands of everyday life, but there are techniques that can quiet the mind and help us answer—or at least begin to ask—the kinds of deep questions people have been asking themselves throughout history. Why am I here? What is my purpose? Who do I want to be?

Some find meaning in religion or spirituality, especially in the act of prayer. Prayer can help us feel less alone, more connected, and more resilient. It can't solve the world's problems, but it can give us inner strength and even support our mental health: a Baylor University study found that people who pray to a loving God are less likely to experience anxiety-related disorders.

> ## HOW I THRIVE
>
> **VICTORIA ARLEN**, ESPN sportscaster
>
> **Anytime you feel burned out, take a moment to meditate or pray.**
>
> "It usually involves shutting off for a moment. Either going to the lake or the ocean and just having time to meditate and pray and take in everything."
>
> • • • •

Agapi Stassinopoulos, an author, inspirational speaker, and Thrive Global facilitator (and also Arianna's sister), provides insight into this phenomenon: "It's amazing how simply stopping for a moment and trusting that you can ask for help can make a difference," she says. "People typically associate prayer with religion, but it's really an internal request for help and a moment of gratitude. It is the golden bridge between us, our worldly human self and the wise, loving intelligence in us. This golden bridge is available to us 24-7."

Meditation is another practice that can help us connect to our purpose. Arianna calls it a "miracle drug," with side effects, including more focus, better memory, longer attention span, enhanced creativity, and greater well-being.

Every element of well-being is enhanced by the practice of meditation, and, indeed, studies have shown that mindfulness and meditation have a measurable positive impact on everything we've been exploring: wisdom, wonder, and giving. As Jon Kabat-Zinn, founding director of the Stress Reduction Clinic and the Center for Mindfulness at the University of Massachusetts Medical School, writes, "In all Asian languages, the word for 'mind' and the word for 'heart' are the same words. So when we hear the word 'mindfulness,' we have to inwardly also hear 'heartfulness' in order to grasp it even as a concept, and especially as a way of being." In other words, mindfulness is not just about our minds but our whole beings.

Almost anything can be done mindfully. Just practice paying attention to whatever you are doing at any given moment: brushing your teeth, drinking coffee, or taking a shower. Focus on the rising and falling of your breath for ten seconds. Pausing several times a day to simply breathe allows you to feel less tense and be more present in your life.

Many of the world's most successful public figures, from philanthropists and business leaders to musicians and actors, have experienced the benefits of meditation.

For singer Katy Perry, meditating for twenty minutes delivers a powerful energy shift. "It shifts my whole mood," she says. "I find this inner joy again."

Melinda Gates makes it a habit too. "Investing even a few minutes in meditation makes the whole day happier and more productive. . . . No matter where I am in the world, that one's pretty nonnegotiable." Notably, Gates sees deep benefits from short bursts of mindfulness. "I'll do just a three- or five-minute meditation," she tells Thrive. "We don't always have 20 minutes to meditate, but I learned from a great meditation teacher that if you just sit in small increments throughout the day, those moments will add up like pearls on a string. By the end of the day, you have a string of beautiful pearls. And that's really helped me."

Meditation also physically changes our brains. Dr. Richard Davidson, professor of psychiatry at the University of Wisconsin–Madison and a leading scholar on the impact of contemplative practices on the brain, used magnetic resonance imaging machines (MRIs) to study the brain activity of Tibetan monks. The studies, as Davidson put it, have illuminated for the first time the "further reaches of human plasticity and transformation." He describes meditation as mental training: "What we found is that the trained mind, or brain, is physically different from the untrained one." And when our brain is changed, so is the way in which we experience the world.

"Meditation is not just blissing out under a mango tree," says French Buddhist monk and molecular geneticist Matthieu Ricard. "It completely changes your brain and therefore changes what you are." And this automatically changes how you respond to what is happening in your life, your level of stress, and your ability to tap into your wisdom when making decisions. "You don't learn to sail in stormy seas," Ricard says. "You go to a secluded place, not to avoid the world, but to avoid distractions until you build your strength and you can deal with anything."

It's hard to think of anything else that is simultaneously so simple and so powerful. It's important to recognize that our Western traditions of prayer and contemplation, and the Stoic philosophy of ancient Greece and Rome, fulfill the same purpose as the Eastern practice of meditation. According to Taoist philosophy, "Rest is prior to motion and stillness prior to action." And, returning to spirituality, every Christian tradition incorporates some equivalent form of mindfulness. For example, in the sixth century, Saint Benedict established the tradition of Lectio Divina ("divine reading"), a four-part practice of reading, meditation, prayer, and contemplation.

FINDING MEANING IN TIMES OF ADVERSITY AND TRANSITION

Very often, life's most difficult experiences end up being the most meaningful. When we're up against challenges, we find out who we are, what we value, and what we're capable of.

The COVID-19 pandemic is a dramatic example, and also one of the most instructive. The challenges of this time have forced each of us to discover that certain parts of life were not as essential as we thought—and just as important, rediscover certain essential parts we had forgotten. As Pope Francis said in the blessing he delivered while praying for an end to the coronavirus, "It is a time to choose what matters and what passes away, a time to separate what is necessary from what is not."

Bruce Feiler explores just how meaningful these moments of transition and adversity can be in his 2020 book, *Life Is in the Transitions: Mastering Change at Any Age.* As Feiler notes, life is never the linear path we might expect or want it to be. We are always going to have disruptions. What has changed is that the number of disruptions is increasing. And since life transitions are both inevitable and increasing, Feiler asks: "Why do we insist on talking about these periods as something dire and defeating, as miserable slogs we have to grit, grind, or grovel our way through? As long as life is going to be full of plot twists, why not spend more time learning to master them?"

The key to coming through these transitions, and the bigger changes Feiler calls "lifequakes," stronger than before is to use the time of disruption to connect with the core of who we are. "Perhaps the most important thing I learned in more than a thousand hours of interviews," Feiler writes, "is that a life transition is a meaning-making exercise."

Whether the transition is voluntary or involuntary, personal or collective, these periods, in which we become "exiles from the normal boundaries of life," involve shedding and purging. That's what connecting with the sacred in our lives is all about: sacrifice, renewal, and rebirth. As Feiler puts it, "*I used to be that. Then I went through a change. Now I am this.*"

One of the keys to getting the most out of our transitions— and our lives in general—is to understand our lives as stories, which Feiler calls "the primary psychic unit of being alive," making us "more human and more humane." Stories are how we think and dream. Stories are how we make sense of the world, and of the past, present, and future. Stories are how we connect with others and with ourselves. That's why life transitions can seem so threatening. "A breach in narrative is an existential event," Feiler writes.

But life transitions also give us a chance to reflect and "fix the plot holes in our life stories." Feiler writes that transitions are "an autobiographical occasion, when we simply must take the opportunity to revisit, revise, and ultimately restart our internal autobiographies, making some tweaks, adding a new chapter or two, elevating or devaluing certain themes."

One powerful Microstep is to simply write your own story. Feiler recounts a famous 1986 study by James Pennebaker of the University of Texas at Austin. Pennebaker asked a group of students to write about traumatic experiences in their lives for fifteen minutes each evening for four consecutive nights. Though the writing experience was difficult—many cried during the process—one year later, the students had fewer visits to the health center and 70 percent said they understood themselves better. Follow-up studies even showed signs of a stronger immune system.

The key about successful transitions is that they are more about meaning than about happiness: "Happiness is fleeting," he writes, "while meaning is enduring; happiness concentrates on the self while meaning concentrates on things larger than the self; happiness focuses on the present while meaning focuses on stitching together the past, present, and future."

FOLLOWING OUR INTUITION

Another pathway to meaning involves following our intuition—our inner voice that is always there, always reading the situation, always trying to steer us in the right direction. But are we listening? Are we paying attention?

Before we dismiss intuition as a private, fully interior phenomenon that doesn't translate to the real world, let's consider how important it has been to some of history's greatest thinkers. Albert Einstein said: "Intuition, not intellect, is the 'open sesame' of yourself." The third-century philosopher Plotinus wrote that there are three degrees of knowledge: "opinion, science, illumination. The means or instrument of the first is sense; of the second, dialectic; of the third, intuition." The internet has made the first two types of knowledge very easy to come by. But it has taken us further away from that illumination, or wisdom, that is essential to living a life that matters.

Science has confirmed how important intuition is in the way we make decisions. "It has long been realized," psychologists Martin Seligman and Michael Kahana wrote, "that many important decisions are not arrived at by linear reasoning, but by intuition." There's a reason why we feel that our intuition comes from deep inside—why it's referred to sometimes as a "gut instinct" or a "feeling in your bones." It's because intuition is part of the core of our internal wiring.

In a world of data sets and algorithms that make decisions for us, tuning into our intuition is harder than ever. But when we're intentional about checking in with ourselves, even for just a few minutes a day, we can tap into our own internal wisdom and let our intuition guide us toward the good life. Next time you're on the fence or struggling with a decision—however small—ask yourself what feels right, and then go with it. You'll build your intuition muscle and see that trusting your gut can lead to great decisions.

THE EYE OF THE HURRICANE

When Arianna Huffington delivered the commencement speech to the class of 2013 at Smith College, she ended with the words, "Onward, upward, and inward!" And if there is one overarching theme to this book, it is that we cannot thrive and lead the lives we want (as opposed to lives we settle for) without learning to go inward. Whatever our goals, wherever we are in life, the challenges we face are steep, but each of us has within us the qualities we need to truly thrive.

But how can we tap into these qualities when our frenetic, breathless lives seem designed to keep us from doing so?

One metaphor that can guide us is the eye of the hurricane— that centered place of strength, wisdom, and peace that we all have inside ourselves. This was the place that Marcus Aurelius, the emperor of Rome for nineteen years—facing plagues, invasions, and betrayals—described in his book *Meditations*.

A fundamental truth is that we're all going to veer away from that centered place again and again and again. That's the nature of life. In fact, we may be off course more often than we are on course.

The question is how quickly we can get back to that centered place. How can we bypass the collective delusion that burnout is simply the price we must pay for success? How can we show up ready to live and lead from what is best, wisest, most creative, and empathetic in us?

Let's remember what airline attendants instruct us to do in the case of an emergency: put our own oxygen mask on first. If we follow this advice, then we'll be most able to help others during times of trouble.

When we accept that it's the quality—not the quantity—of our decisions that really matters, it becomes easier for us to see the stakes of the impaired decision-making that comes from not taking time to recharge. Athletes were the first to recognize that recovery is an essential part of peak performance. The same is true for the less athletically gifted among us: we can't perform at our best if we forgo sleep, overindulge in stress eating, soothe our anxiety and uncertainty with alcohol, or—does this sound too familiar?—forget to take even a minute to move between back-to-back Zoom meetings.

When we do take care of ourselves, we see benefits to our physical and mental health, performance, and productivity. When we don't, we pay a price: innovation, creativity, resilience, empathy, decision-making, and team building are the first to disappear when we are burned out and depleted. In order to access our deepest wisdom, our brilliant creativity, and our compassion, we need to commit to taking care of ourselves. And that entails getting into the eye of the hurricane so we can experience life's deeper wonders, like meaning and fulfillment. If we do that incrementally in small ways, we can transform ourselves and our communities, step-by-step.

MICROSTEP DIARY

Kasia Laskowski, executive director, Thrive Global Foundation

MICROSTEP: Set aside just a few minutes each night to write in a journal.

Why I Chose It

I used to journal each morning, but my long commute makes finding this time increasingly difficult. I hope that by incorporating this Microstep into my evenings, I can build this writing ritual back into my routine, even if it is only for a few minutes.

What Happened

For the first few weeks, I wrote in my journal every night, even if it was just a few words. Toward the end of the Microstep period, I caught a pretty bad cold so I found it hard to keep up with my Microstep during this week; I couldn't seem to keep on schedule. That said, I would find other times during the day where I could fit in time to write.

I sleep more soundly after I journal. There is something quite calming and relaxing about reflecting on my day and writing down all the lingering thoughts and concerns. Some nights, it felt as if a weight was being lifted off my shoulders. As I closed my notebook, I gave myself permission to release that which I could not control.

Thirteen days after I began my challenge, I wrote the first poem I had written in probably six months. It was as if muscle memory sparked the creativity and resulted in a benefit I did not expect.

There was a situation that came up in which I was having trouble communicating with my boyfriend. I wrote down everything I wanted to talk through. This allowed me to feel more confident and prepared for our next conversation and actually helped us to both connect and understand each other in a new way.

MICROSTEPS

Pick a time each day to compliment a coworker on a job well done. It's a great way to show gratitude, which strengthens relationships and boosts resilience.

Whenever you're about to do some demanding work, take a moment to think about how it will make someone's life easier or have some other positive effect. Reframing in these moments when work gets tough can give you a deeper sense of meaning and help you stay motivated.

Listen to your intuition. Next time you're on the fence or struggling with a decision—however small—ask yourself what feels right, and then go with it. You'll build your intuition muscle and see that trusting your gut can lead to great decisions.

Focus on the rising and falling of your breath for ten seconds. Pausing several times a day to simply breathe allows you to feel less tense and be more present in your life.

Say thank you. Gratitude is one of the most powerful emotions, with benefits that extend both inward and outward. And it often starts with taking a moment to be grateful for this day, for being alive, for anything.

Use a skill or talent you have to help someone who could benefit from it. Giving back has been proven to boost our sense of purpose and well-being. It jump-starts your transition from a go-getter to a go-giver, and reconnects you to the world and to the natural abundance in your own life.

After completing a project, write an email thanking a colleague (or your whole team) for their support. The simple act of putting your gratitude in writing will strengthen your relationships with coworkers and allow you to reflect on how much their support helped you before you move on to the next task.

Give credit where it's due. Whether in front of a group or one-on-one, few things motivate people as much as being recognized for their contributions. It's a form of generosity that reflects well on you, and it feels great.

Take just five minutes to write a list of your values. Ask yourself, "What matters most to me?" and then jot down your thoughts in a notebook or on a sticky note. Better yet, post your list at your desk so you can revisit it and add to it at the start of each week.

Take advantage of moments of micro-rest. Next time you feel stressed or tired, take a minute to stretch or breathe deeply instead of scrolling through social media or grabbing an unhealthy snack. You'll reduce your stress and set yourself up to be more energetic and productive when you get back to work.

HOW YOU CAN THRIVE

Think back to a difficult experience you've had in your life that you now consider meaningful. What was it, and how did it create a sense of meaning in your life?

Now, think about a challenge you're currently going through. How are you growing or learning in meaningful ways you might not have previously considered?

What are some limiting beliefs you have around living a life of meaning and purpose? For example, *I'm just one person so I can't make a real difference* or *The work I do is meaningless.*

Take a moment to reflect on the meaning and impact of the work you do. What do you create? Who do you create it for? What impact does it have?

Did any of the science or stories in this chapter help you think differently about giving, gratitude, or intuition?

What's one Microstep you can implement today to be a part of something larger than yourself or infuse more purpose into your life?

ACKNOWLEDGMENTS

In these pages we've explored the power of gratitude, and now's my chance to share my own gratitude for all the people who made this book possible.

To Pilar Queen and Albert Lee, for being true believers in Thrive's mission and message, and working to make sure that message reaches and helps as many people as possible.

To the Hachette Go team, for being our partners at every stage of bringing this book to life: Mary Ann Naples, Renee Sedliar, Michael Clark, Mike van Mantgem, Michelle Aielli, Michael Barrs, Sarah Falter, Alison Dalafave, and Amber Hoover.

To my Thrive colleagues and friends, for their editorial insights and absolute commitment to bringing the very best of Thrive to these pages: Gregory Beyer, Alexandra Hayes Robinson, Margarita Bertsos, Elaine Lipworth, Stephen Sherrill, Danny Shea, Mallory Stratton, and Ksenia Kirilyuk.

To the many friends of Thrive—researchers, experts, business leaders, entertainers, thought leaders, and community members—whose contributions and stories made this book even richer.

And finally, to Arianna Huffington, whose relentless commitment to changing the way we work and live is the guiding spirit of this book.

REFERENCES

FOREWORD BY ARIANNA HUFFINGTON

x **Duke University:** David T. Neal, Wendy Wood, and Jeffrey M. Quinn, "Habits—a Repeat Performance," *Current Directions in Psychological Science* 15, no. 4 (2006), https://dornsife.usc.edu/assets/sites/545/docs/Wendy_Wood_Research_Articles/Habits/Neal.Wood.Quinn.2006_Habits_a_repeat_performance.pdf.

x *Willpower:* Roy F. Baumeister and John Tierney, *Willpower: Rediscovering the Greatest Human Strength* (New York: Penguin, 2011).

x *Atomic Habits:* James Clear, *Atomic Habits: An Easy & Proven Way to Build Good Habits & Break Bad Ones* (New York: Avery, 2018).

xi **Fogg:** "How to Make Healthy Life Changes from Tiny Habits," *WRVO Public Media* (August 13, 2016), https://www.wrvo.org/post/how-make-healthy-life-changes-tiny-habits.

xi *Tiny Habits:* BJ Fogg, *Tiny Habits: The Small Changes That Change Everything* (Boston: Houghton Mifflin Harcourt, 2020).

xii **sixty to ninety seconds:** Jennifer R. Piazza, Susan T. Charles, Martin J. Sliwinski, Jacqueline Mogle, and David M. Almeida, "Affective Reactivity to Daily Stressors and Long-Term Risk of Reporting a Chronic Physical Health Condition," *Annals of*

Behavioral Medicine 45, no. 1 (February 2013): 110–120, https://academic.oup.com/abm/article-abstract/45/1/110 /4563898?redirectedFrom=fulltext.

CHAPTER 1: SLEEP

2   **"Keystone habits":** Charles Duhigg, "The Habit Loop," *The Power of Habit: Why We Do What We Do in Life and Business* (New York: Random House, 2012), 100–101.

4   **Tiffany Cruikshank:** Linsey Benoit O'Connell, "Rise and Thrive with Tiffany Cruikshank, the Founder of Yoga Medicine," Thrive Global (August 2, 2019), https://thriveglobal .com/stories/thrive-questionnaire-tiffany-cruikshank -morning-routine-sleep-tips/.

5   **Baba Shiv:** Baba Shiv, "The Most Fascinating Thing That Happens in Your Brain While You're Sleeping," Thrive Global (October 18, 2019), https://thriveglobal.com/stories/mental -health-deep-slow-wave-sleep-brain-science-emotion-decision -making/.

6   **"like a dishwasher":** Jon Hamilton, "Brains Sweep Themselves Clean of Toxins During Sleep," *All Things Considered*, NPR (October 17, 2013), https://www.npr.org/sections/health-shots /2013/10/18/236211811/brains-sweep-themselves-clean-of -toxins-during-sleep.

6   **"Even a soul submerged in sleep":** Heraclitus, *Fragments: The Collected Wisdom of Heraclitus*, trans. Brooks Haxton (New York: Viking, 2001), Kindle edition.

6   **In fact, skimping on sleep:** A. M. Williamson and Anne-Marie Feyer, "Moderate Sleep Deprivation Produces Impairments in Cognitive and Motor Performance Equivalent to Legally Prescribed Levels of Alcohol Intoxication," *Occupational and Environmental Medicine* 57 (2000): 649–655.

6   **A study from Karolinska Institutet:** "A Sleep-Deprived Brain Interprets Impressions Negatively," Karolinska Institutet

(April 18, 2019), https://news.ki.se/a-sleep-deprived-brain -interprets-impressions-negatively.

7   **Michael Phelps:** Jill Rosen, "Michael Phelps and His High-Altitude Sleeping Chamber," *Baltimore Sun* (May 7, 2012), https://www.baltimoresun.com/features/bs-xpm-2012 -05-07-bal-michael-phelps-bed-20120507-story.html.

7   **"an alert stimulus":** Laura Beil, "In Eyes, a Clock Calibrated by Wavelengths of Light," *New York Times* (July 4, 2011), https://www.nytimes.com/2011/07/05/health/05light.html.

8   **For American adults, 88 percent admit:** "New Survey: 88% of US Adults Lose Sleep Due to Binge-Watching," *American Academy of Sleep Medicine* (November 4, 2019), https://aasm .org/sleep-survey-binge-watching-results.

8   **the National Sleep Foundation recommends:** "How to Sleep When It's Hot Outside," SleepFoundation.org (October 2, 2020), https://www.sleepfoundation.org/articles/sleeping-when -it-blistering-hot.

8   **Tom Brady:** Tom Brady, "Tom Brady: 'My Wife Doesn't Even Allow Cell Phones Near the Bed When We Sleep,'" Thrive Global (September 19, 2017), https://thriveglobal.com/ stories/tom-brady-my-wife-doesn-t-even-allow-cell -phones-near-the-bed-when-we-sleep/.

8   **"We have this illusion":** A. Pawlowski, "Why Eating Late at Night May Be Bad for Your Brain," *TODAY* (February 22, 2015), https://www.today.com/health/eating-late-night-may -disrupt-learning-memory-t4576.

9   **Tamron Hall:** Tamron Hall, "Television Anchor Tamron Hall on Energizing with Afternoon Naps," Thrive Global (November 30, 2016), https://thriveglobal.com/stories/nbc-s -tamron-hall-on-energizing-with-afternoon-naps/.

10 **"Over the course of the day":** Stephanie Fairyington, "Good Sleep Starts the Moment You Wake Up," Thrive Global (May 10, 2019), https://thriveglobal.com/stories/good-sleep -prepare-during-day-tips-calming-relaxing/.

10   **University of Pennsylvania researchers:** Greg Richter, "Yoga, Running, Weight Lifting, and Gardening: Penn Study Maps the Types of Physical Activity Associated with Better Sleep Habits," *Penn Today* (June 4, 2015), https://penntoday.upenn.edu/news/yoga-running-weight-lifting-and-gardening-penn-study-maps-types-physical-activity-associated-be.

11   **Matthew Walker:** Matthew Walker, *Why We Sleep: Unlocking the Power of Sleep and Dreams* (New York: Scribner, 2017), 3–11.

11   **According to David Randall:** David K. Randall, "Rethinking Sleep," *New York Times* (September 22, 2012), https://www.nytimes.com/2012/09/23/opinion/sunday/rethinking-sleep.html.

12   **Hoda Kotb:** Stephanie Fairyington, "Hoda Kotb's Research-Backed Self-Care Routine Can Dramatically Improve Your Life," Thrive Global (November 9, 2018), https://thriveglobal.com/stories/hoda-kotbs-research-backed-self-care-routine-can-dramatically-improve-your-life/.

12   **Jeff Bezos told Thrive:** Jeff Bezos, "Why Getting 8 Hours of Sleep Is Good for Amazon Shareholders," Thrive Global (November 30, 2016), https://thriveglobal.com/stories/jeff-bezos-why-getting-8-hours-of-sleep-is-good-for-amazon-shareholders/.

13   **And as Kristin Lemkau:** Kristin Lemkau, "J.P. Morgan CMO: How I Learned to Put My Own Oxygen Mask on First," Thrive Global (November 30, 2016), https://thriveglobal.com/stories/j-p-morgan-cmo-how-i-learned-to-put-my-own-oxygen-mask-on-first/.

13   **Reid Hoffman:** Stephanie Fairyington, "Jeff Bezos Says Prioritizing This One Habit Is Key to His Success," Thrive Global (October 30, 2018), https://thriveglobal.com/stories/jeff-bezos-says-prioritizing-this-one-habit-is-key-to-his-success/.

13 **Olympic gold medalist Mikaela Shiffrin's:** Nick Paumgarten, "Mikaela Shiffrin, the Best Slalom Skier in the World," *New Yorker* (November 27, 2017), https://www.newyorker.com /magazine/2017/11/27/mikaela-shiffrin-the-best-slalom -skier-in-the-world.

14 **Shelly Ibach:** Shelly Ibach, "Sleep Better: How to Fall Back Asleep When You Wake Up Too Early," Thrive Global (August 16, 2019), https://thriveglobal.com/stories/sleep-better -tips-how-to-get-back-to-sleep-wake-early/.

14 **"My pre-bed routine":** Thrive Global, "How Andre Iguodala Trains His Body, Mind and Soul," Facebook, November, 29, 2016, https://www.facebook.com/thriveglbl/videos/how-andre -iguodala-trains-his-body-mind-and-soul/225771667844659/.

15 **John Steinbeck:** John Steinbeck, *Sweet Thursday* (New York: Penguin, [1954] 1979), 107.

16 **Microstep Diary, Clarice Metzger:** Clarice Metzger, "I Set a Bedtime Alarm Every Day for 32 Days and Here's What Happened," Thrive Global (November 6, 2019), https://thrive global.com/stories/bedtime-alarm-sleep-ritual-microstep -diary/.

CHAPTER 2: UNPLUGGING AND RECHARGING

22 **Michelle Phan:** Lindsey Benoit O'Connell, "Why Michelle Phan Thinks Being Alone Is So Important," Thrive Global (October 18, 2019), https://thriveglobal.com/stories/michelle -phan-beauty-entrepreneur-youtube-star-alone-time-burn out-hiatus/.

23 **electric shock:** Timothy D. Wilson, David A. Reinhard, Erin C. Westgate, Daniel T. Gilbert, Nicole Ellerbeck, Cheryl Hahn, Casey L. Brown, and Adi Shaked, "Just Think: The Challenges of the Disengaged Mind," *Science* (July 2014): 75–77, https://science.sciencemag.org/content/345/6192/75.long.

24   **86 percent of Americans:** American Psychological Association "Stress in America" poll, "APA's Survey Finds Constantly Checking Electronic Devices Linked to Significant Stress for Most Americans" (February 23, 2017), https://www.apa.org /news/press/releases/2017/02/checking-devices.

24   **Elon Musk:** David Gelles, James B. Stewart, Jessica Silver-Greenberg, and Kate Kelly, "Elon Musk Details 'Excruciating' Personal Toll of Tesla Turmoil," *New York Times* (April 16, 2018), https://www.nytimes.com/2018/08/16/business/elon -musk-interview-tesla.html.

24   **Demi Moore:** Lindsey Benoit O'Connell, "Demi Moore on Her Morning Routine," Thrive Global (October 7, 2019), https://thriveglobal.com/stories/demi-moore-morning -routine-ritual-self-care/.

24   **Overwork:** Claire Cain Miller, "Women Did Everything Right. Then Work Got 'Greedy,'" *New York Times* (April 26, 2019), https://www.nytimes.com/2019/04/26/upshot/women -long-hours-greedy-professions.html.

25   **Philipp Schindler:** Philipp Schindler, "Google's Chief Business Officer Talks About His Wake-Up Call," Thrive Global (December 11; 2017), https://thriveglobal.com/stories/google -chief-business-officer-talks-about-his-wake-up-call/.

25   **Data from LinkedIn:** Blair Heitmann, "Timely Tips for Navigating the Holidays Like a Pro," *LinkedIn Official Blog* (December 10, 2018), https://blog.linkedin.com/2018/december /10/timely-tips-for-navigating-the-holidays-like-a-pro.

25   **presenteeism:** Douglas Broom, "Working When Sick Is Rising and Harms You and Your Employer. This Is Why," World Economic Forum (May 2, 2019), https://www.weforum.org /agenda/2019/05/working-when-sick-is-rising-and-harms -you-and-your-employer-this-is-why/.

26   **Mark Cuban:** "Mark Cuban," *Thrive Global Podcast* (April 18, 2018), https://thriveglobal.com/stories/the-thrive -global-podcast-episode-3-mark-cuban/.

26 **absolutely no reduction in stress:** Susan J. Young, "Returning from Vacation Doesn't Ensure Less Stress, New Fierce Survey Finds," Travel Agent Central (January 21, 2017), https://www.travelagentcentral.com/running-your-business/embargoed-fierce-vacation-survey.

27 **last social gathering:** Lee Rainie and Kathryn Zickuhr, "Americans' Views on Mobile Etiquette," Pew Research Center, Internet and Technology (August 26, 2015), https://www.pewresearch.org/internet/2015/08/26/americans-views-on-mobile-etiquette/.

27 **When two people are in a conversation:** Andrew K. Przybylski and Netta Weinstein, "Can You Connect with Me Now? How the Presence of Mobile Communication Technology Influences Face-to-Face Conversation Quality," *Journal of Social and Personal Relationships* 30, no. 3 (July 2012), https://journals.sagepub.com/doi/10.1177/0265407512453827.

27 **Jennifer Aniston:** Kelsey Murray and Jennifer Aniston: "If 'Friends' Was Created Today, You Would Have a Coffee Shop Full of People That Were Just Staring into iPhones," Thrive Global (May 10, 2017), https://thriveglobal.com/stories/jennifer-aniston-if-friends-was-created-today-you-would-have-a-coffee-shop-full-of-people-that-were-just-staring-into-iphones/.

28 **150 times a day:** James Roberts and Stephen Pirog, "A Preliminary Investigation of Materialism and Impulsiveness as Predictors of Technological Addictions Among Young Adults," *Journal of Behavioral Addictions* 2, no. 1 (2012): 56–62, https://akjournals.com/view/journals/2006/2/1/article-p56.xml.

28 **backing away from our phones:** Monideepa Tarafdar, Christian Maier, Sven Laumer, and Tim Weitzel, "Explaining the Link Between Technostress and Technology Addiction for Social Networking Sites: A Study of Distraction as a Coping Behavior," *Wiley Online Library* (August 27, 2019), https://onlinelibrary.wiley.com/doi/abs/10.1111/isj.12253.

28 **Phubbing:** James A. Roberts and Meredith E. David, "My Life Has Become a Major Distraction from My Cell Phone: Partner Phubbing and Relationship Satisfaction Among Romantic Partners," *Computers in Human Behavior* 54 (January 2016): 134–141, https://www.sciencedirect.com/science/article/abs/pii/S0747563215300704?via%3Dihub.

28 **negatively impacting their relationship:** Brandon T. McDaniel and Sarah M. Coyne, "'Technoference': The Interference of Technology in Couple Relationships and Implications for Women's Personal and Relational Well-Being," *Psychology of Popular Media Culture 5*, no. 1 (2016): 85–98, https://doi.org/10.1037/ppm0000065.

29 **Suzy Batiz:** Lindsey Benoit O'Connell, "Entrepreneur Suzy Batiz Prioritizes Mental Health to Achieve Business Success," Thrive Global (October 9, 2019), https://thriveglobal.com/stories/entrepreneur-suzy-baitz-priorities-mental-health-business-success/.

29 **World Health Organization:** "Burn-Out an 'Occupational Phenomenon': International Classification of Diseases," World Health Organization (May 28, 2019), https://www.who.int/mental_health/evidence/burn-out/en/.

29 **reported feeling burned out:** Ben Wigert and Sangeeta Agrawal, "Employee Burnout, Part 1: The 5 Main Causes," Gallup (July 12, 2018), https://www.gallup.com/workplace/237059/employee-burnout-part-main-causes.aspx.

29 **Bonnie Tsui:** Bonnie Tsui, "You Are Doing Something Important When You Aren't Doing Anything," *New York Times* (June 21, 2019), https://www.nytimes.com/2019/06/21/opinion/summer-lying-fallow.html.

30 **Aarón Sánchez:** Aarón Sánchez, "MasterChef's Aarón Sánchez on Staying Connected to His Roots," Thrive Global (August 18, 2017), https://thriveglobal.com/stories/aaron-sanchez-on-staying-connected-to-his-roots/.

30 **Alex Soojung-Kim Pang:** Alex Soojung-Kim Pang, *Rest: Why You Get More Done When You Work Less* (New York: Basic Books, 2016).

32 **"experiments in asceticism":** Casey Cep, "The Pointlessness of Unplugging," *New Yorker* (March 19, 2014), https://www.newyorker.com/culture/culture-desk/the-pointlessness-of-unplugging.

32 **"going offline is a struggle":** Fotini Markopoulou, "How I Manage My Stress," Thrive Global (October 9, 2019), https://thriveglobal.com/stories/how-i-manage-my-stress/.

33 **Nir Eyal:** Nir Eyal, *Indistractable: How to Control Your Attention and Choose Your Life* (London: Bloomsbury, 2020).

33 **Mike Posner:** Mike Posner, "Mike Posner: End Goals Are Overrated," Thrive Global (June 14, 2017), https://thriveglobal.com/stories/mike-posner-end-goals-are-overrated/.

33 **Lori Gottlieb:** Lori Gottlieb, *Maybe You Should Talk to Someone* (Boston: Houghton Mifflin Harcourt, 2019).

34 **"being chained to your mobile phone":** BJ Fogg (@bjfogg), "A Movement to Be 'Post-Digital' Will Emerge in 2020," Twitter, September 11, 2019, https://twitter.com/bjfogg/status/1171883692488183809.

34 **Andre Iguodala:** Rebecca Muller, "How Jennifer Aniston and Other Celebrities Prioritize Their Happiness by Unplugging," Thrive Global (February 21, 2010), https://thriveglobal.com/stories/jennifer-aniston-other-celebrities-prioritize-unplugging/.

36 **Microstep Diary, Lisa Chin Mollica:** Lisa Chin Mollica, "I Put My Phone on Night Shift for 32 Days and Here's What Happened," Thrive Global (November 6, 2019), https://thriveglobal.com/storiesphone-night-shift-mode-microstep-diary/.

42 **"Don't eat anything your great-grandmother"**: Charles Matthews, "Just Eat What Your Great-Grandma Ate," *San Francisco Chronicle*, Michael Pollan (December 30, 2007), https://michaelpollan.com/reviews/just-eat-what-your-great-grandma-ate/.

43 **"Our fast-paced, high-stress lives"**: Maya Adam, "Asking Yourself These Two Questions Will Transform Your Approach to Eating," Thrive Global (October 10, 2019), https://thriveglobal.com/stories/mental-health-food-choices-approach-eating-how-to-questions-ask/.

44 **"We're easily blinded"**: Arushi Mehta, "Young Entrepreneurs Are Notoriously Unhealthy," *YSF Magazine* (January 13, 2018), https://yfsmagazine.com/2018/01/13/young-entrepreneurs-are-notoriously-unhealthy/.

44 **Michelle Obama:** "First Lady Michelle Obama on Healthy Eating Habits and More," Everyday Health, n.d., https://www.everydayhealth.com/diet-and-nutrition-pictures/first-lady-michelle-obama-on-healthy-eating-habits-and-more.aspx.

44 **"Expectations for health are so low"**: Shalini Ramachandran and Rolfe Winkler, "Beyond the Confetti: The Dark Side of Startup Success," *Wall Street Journal* (July 12, 2019), https://www.wsj.com/articles/beyond-the-confetti-the-dark-side-of-startup-success-11562923804.

44 **"I'm trying to spread the word"**: Anne Cassidy, "A Former Diet Cola Addict Built a $100m Firm," BBC (September 29, 2019), https://www.bbc.com/news/business-49811129.

45 **"I wasn't eating well, drinking enough water"**: Dreamers & Doers, "15 Stories of Burnout from Successful Female CEOs, Founders, and Leaders, and Their Advice for Avoiding the Same Fate," *Business Insider* (February 2, 2020), https://www

.businessinsider.com/female-ceos-founders-leaders-burnout
-confessions-advice.

45 **Maria Menounos:** Lindsey Benoit O'Connell, "Maria Menounos: 'I'm on a Journey to Keep Getting Better,'" Thrive
Global (October 16, 2019), https://thriveglobal.com/stories
/maria-menounos-mental-health-morning-routine/.

45 **"I began to see the pattern we were in":** Michelle Obama,
"Chapter 16," *Becoming* (New York: Crown Publishing, 2018).

46 **One Brigham Young University study of nearly 20,000:**
Ray M. Merrill, Steven G. Aldana, James E. Pope, David R.
Anderson, and Carter Coberley, "Presenteeism According to
Healthy Behaviors, Physical Health, and Work Environment,"
Population Health Management 15 (2012): 293–301, https://
www.researchgate.net/publication/230628613_Presenteeism
_According_to_Healthy_Behaviors_Physical_Health_and
_Work_Environment.

47 **Bianca Bosker:** Thrive Global, "Bianca Bosker: 'I've Become
Militantly Protective About Bedtime,'" Thrive Global (March
24, 2017), https://thriveglobal.com/stories/bianca-bosker-i-ve
-become-militantly-protective-about-bedtime/.

47 **Caffeine has a half-life of five to six hours:** K. Sepkowitz,
"Energy Drinks and Caffeine-Related Adverse Effects," *Journal of the American Medical Association* 309 (2013): 243–244,
https://www.semanticscholar.org/paper/Energy-drinks
-and-caffeine-related-adverse-effects.-Sepkowitz/b01c37d
688562a0bd769853b7ff50d312b0b4788?p2df.

48 **Ashley Wilking:** Ashley Wilking, "Ashley Wilking on the
Question She Asks Herself Every Single Day," Thrive Global
(April 26, 2017), https://thriveglobal.com/stories/ashley
-wilking-on-the-question-she-asks-herself-every-single-day/.

48 **"This analogy is misleading":** Ron Friedman, "What You Eat
Affects Your Productivity," *Harvard Business Review* (October 17, 2014), https://hbr.org/2014/10/what-you-eat-affects
-your-productivity.

49   "Americans routinely change what they eat": Richard Schiff-
      man, "Eat Better, Feel Better? Food Advice from the Year in
      Well," *New York Times* (January 1, 2020), https://www.ny
      times.com/2020/01/01/well/eat/eat-better-feel-better-food
      -advice-from-the-year-in-well.html.

49   **Poor eating habits have been linked to common mental dis-
      orders including depression and anxiety:** T. S. Sathyanarayana
      Rao, M. R. Asha, et al., "Understanding Nutrition, Depres-
      sion and Mental Illnesses," *Indian Journal of Psychiatry* 50,
      no. 2 (2008 April–June: 77–82, https://www.ncbi.nlm.nih.gov
      /pmc/articles/PMC2738337/.

49   **Poor eating habits have been linked to common mental dis-
      orders including depression and anxiety:** Kelli Miller, "Can
      What You Eat Affect Your Mental Health?," WebMD (Au-
      gust 20, 2015), https://www.webmd.com/mental-health/news
      /20150820/food-mental-health#1.

49   **Poor eating habits have been linked to common mental disor-
      ders including depression and anxiety:** Agnès Le Port, Alice
      Gueguen, et al., "Association Between Dietary Patterns and
      Depressive Symptoms Over Time: A 10-Year Follow-Up Study
      of the GAZEL Cohort," *PLOS ONE* (December 12, 2012),
      https://journals.plos.org/plosone/article?id=10.1371/journal
      .pone.0051593.

49   **Poor eating habits have been linked to common mental
      disorders including depression and anxiety:** Amy Fleming,
      "Nutritional Psychiatry: Can You Eat Yourself Happier?,"
      Guardian (March 18, 2019), https://www.theguardian.com
      /food/2019/mar/18/can-you-eat-yourself-happier-nutritional
      -psychiatry-mental-health.

49   **In a 2017 study out of Australia's Deakin University:** Fe-
      lice N. Jacka, Adrienne O'Neil, Rachelle Opie, et al., "A Ran-
      domised Controlled Trial of Dietary Improvement for Adults
      with Major Depression (the 'SMILES' trial)," *BMC Medicine*
      15, no. 23 (2017), https://doi.org/10.1186s12916-017-0791-y.

49 **Dambisa Moyo:** Dr. Dambisa Moyo, "Dr. Dambisa Moyo Shares Her Morning Routine," Thrive Global (January 18, 2017), https://thriveglobal.com/stories/dr-dambisa-moyo -shares-her-morning-routine/.

50 **Another study found that people who increased their servings of fruits and vegetables:** Redzo Mujcic and Andrew J. Oswald, "Evolution of Well-Being and Happiness After Increases in Consumption of Fruit and Vegetables," *American Journal of Public Health* 15, no. 23 (2016), https://warwick .ac.uk/fac/soc/economics/intranet/manage/news/ajph_actual _july_2016_fruit_and_veg_oswald_final_proofs.pdf.

50 **Our brains are made up of 75 percent water:** Jianfen Zhang, Na Zhang, Songming Du, et al., "The Effects of Hydration Status on Cognitive Performances Among Young Adults in Hebei, China: A Randomized Controlled Trial (RCT)," *International Journal Environmental Research and Public Health* 15, no. 7 (2018): 1477, https://www.ncbi.nlm.nih.gov/pmc /articles/PMC6068860/.

50 **dehydration can adversely affect concentration, mood, and reasoning:** Matthew Ganio, Lawrence E. Armstrong, Douglas J. Casa, Brendon P. McDermott, et al., "Mild Dehydration Impairs Cognitive Performance and Mood of Men," *British Journal of Nutrition* 106, no. 10 (2011): 1535–1543, https:// www.cambridge.org/core/journals/british-journal-of-nutrition /article/mild-dehydration-impairs-cognitive-performance -and-mood-of-men/3388AB36B8DF73E844C9AD 19271A75BF.

50 **an increase in productivity by as much as 14 percent:** Caroline J. Edmonds, Rosanna Crombie, and Mark R. Gardner, "Subjective Thirst Moderates Changes in Speed of Responding Associated with Water Consumption," *Frontiers in Human Neuroscience* (July 16, 2013), https://www.frontiersin.org /articles/10.3389/fnhum.2013.00363/full.

52 **We actually wake up dehydrated:** "The Connection Between Hydration and Sleep," SleepFoundation.org, n.d., https://www.sleepfoundation.org/articles/connection-between -hydration-and-sleep.

53 **when people feel like they belong at work, they are more productive, motivated:** Karyn Twaronite, "The Surprising Power of Simply Asking Coworkers How They're Doing," *Harvard Business Review* (February 28, 2019), https://hbr.org/2019/02 /the-surprising-power-of-simply-asking-coworkers-how -theyre-doing.

53 **"Food can be a partner that drags you down and depletes your physical and mental health":** Maya Adam, "Asking Yourself These Two Questions Will Transform Your Approach to Eating," Thrive Global (October 10, 2019), https:// thriveglobal.com/stories/mental-health-food-choices -approach-eating-how-to-questions-ask/.

54 **Microstep Diary, Rebecca Lerner:** Rebecca Lerner, "I Set a Daily Caffeine Cutoff for 32 Days and Here's What Happened," Thrive Global (January 18, 2019), https://thriveglobal .com/stories/daily-caffeine-cutoff-microstep-diary-results/.

CHAPTER 4: MOVEMENT

60 **Exercise is scientifically linked to lowered stress levels:** Jesse Allen, "Exercise and Stress Relief," Thrive Global (April 12, 2019), https://thriveglobal.com/stories/exercise-and-stress -relief/.

60 **improved brain function:** Charles H. Hillman, Kirk I. Erickson, and Arthur F. Kramer, "Be Smart, Exercise Your Heart: Exercise Effects on Brain and Cognition," *Nature Reviews Neuroscience* 9 (2008): 58–65, https://doi.org/10.1038/nrn2298.

60 **decreased risk of Alzheimer's disease later in life:** Thierry Paillard, Yves Rolland, and Philipe de Souto Barreto, "Protective Effects of Physical Exercise in Alzheimer's Disease and

Parkinson's Disease: A Narrative Review," *Journal of Clinical Neurology*, 11, no. 3 (July 2015): 212–219, https://doi.org /10.3988/jcn.2015.11.3.212.

61   **World Health Organization:** Regina Guthold, Gretchen A. Stevens, Leanne M. Riley, and Fiona C. Bull, "Worldwide Trends in Insufficient Physical Activity from 2001 to 2016: A Pooled Analysis of 358 Population-Based Surveys with 1.9 Million Participants," *Lancet Global Health* 6, no. 10 (October 1, 2018): E1077–E1086, https://doi.org/10.1016/S2214 -109X(18)30357-7.

62   **Training for an Ironman Triathlon Made Me a Better Entrepreneur:** Ryan Frankel, "How Fitness Made Me a Better Entrepreneur," Thrive Global (September 15, 2020), https:// thriveglobal.com/stories/can-fitness-make-you-a-better -entrepreneur/.

62   **aerobic exercise:** David C. Nieman, Dru A. Henson, Melanie D. Austin, and Wei Sha, "Upper Respiratory Tract Infection Is Reduced in Physically Fit and Active Adults," *British Journal of Sports Medicine* 45, no. 12 (2011): 987–992, http://dx .doi.org/10.1136/bjsm.2010.077875.

62   *British Medical Journal*: Carlos A. Celis-Morales, Donald M. Lyall, Paul Welsh, Jana Anderson, Lewis Steell, Yibing Guo, Reno Maldonado, Daniel F. Mackay, Jill P. Pell, Naveed Sattar, and Jason M. R. Gill, "Association Between Active Commuting and Incident Cardiovascular Disease, Cancer, and Mortality: Prospective Cohort Study," *British Medical Journal* 357 (2017): j1456, https://doi.org/10.1136/bmj.j1456.

63   **making your commute more active:** Jane Burnett, "Commute Wearing You Out? Try Looking at This," Thrive Global (October 23, 2018), https://thriveglobal.com/stories/commute -stress-nature/.

63   **Deepak Chopra:** Lindsey Benoit O'Connell, "Deepak Chopra Wants Us All to Take Risks," Thrive Global (November 13,

2019), https://thriveglobal.com/stories/deepak-chopra-mind
fulness-calm-criticism-technology/.

63 **2018 study that links small bursts of exercise to longevity:**
Gretchen Reynolds, "Those 2-Minute Walk Breaks? They
Add Up," *New York Times* (March 28, 2018), https://www
.nytimes.com/2018/03/28/well/move/walking-exercise
-minutes-death-longevity.html.

64 **2019 study from the Centers for Disease Control and Pre-
vention and the RAND Corporation:** Roland Sturm and
Deborah A. Cohen, "Free Time and Physical Activity Among
Americans 15 Years or Older: Cross-Sectional Analysis of the
American Time Use Survey," *Preventing Chronic Disease* 16
(2019): 190017, http://dx.doi.org/10.5888/pcd16.190017.

64 **Dara Torres:** Dara Torres, "The Thrive Questionnaire with
Dara Torres," Thrive Global (October 7, 2019), https://thrive
global.com/stories/the-thrive-questionnaire-with-dara
-torres-olympian-competition-creativity/.

65 **Mayo Clinic recommends:** Mayo Clinic Staff, "Fitting in
Fitness: Finding Time for Physical Activity," Mayo Clinic
(September 27, 2019), https://www.mayoclinic.org/healthy
-lifestyle/fitness/in-depth/fitness/art-20044531.

65 **American Heart Association updated its guidelines on
physical activity:** Katrina L. Piercy and Richard P. Troiano,
"Physical Activity Guidelines for Americans from the US Department of Health and Human Services," *Circulation: Cardiovascular Quality and Outcomes*, 11, no. 11 (2018), https://doi
.org/10.1161/CIRCOUTCOMES.118.005263.

65 **Boris Kodjoe:** Lindsey Benoit O'Connell, "Spotlight on Actor
and Fitness Expert Boris Kodjoe," Thrive Global (August 20,
2019), https://thriveglobal.com/stories/actor-boris-kodjoe
-morning-workout-healthy-family-fitness/.

65 **fascinating study published in *Health Psychology*:** Octavia H.
Zahrt and Alia J. Crum, "Perceived Physical Activity and
Mortality: Evidence from Three Nationally Representative

U.S. Samples," *Health Psychology* 36 no. 11 (2017): 1017–1025, https://doi.org/10.1037/hea0000531.

66 **How Prioritizing My Well-Being Boosted My Success as a Leader:** Deborah Platt Majoras, "How Prioritizing My Well-Being Boosted My Success as a Leader of a Multinational Company," Thrive Global (February 11, 2019), https://thriveglobal.com/stories/prioritizing-my-own-well-being-boosted-my-success-as-a-leader-of-a-multinational-company/.

67 **motivations for working out:** Allyson G. Box, Yuri Feito, Chris Brown, and Steven J. Petruzzello, "Individual Differences Influence Exercise Behavior: How Personality, Motivation, and Behavioral Regulation Vary Among Exercise Mode Preferences," *Heliyon* 5, no. 4 (April 1, 2019): E01459, https://doi.org/10.1016/j.heliyon.2019.e01459.

67 **Traci Copeland:** Danielle Sinay, "Reach Your Nutrition and Movement Goals with This Advice from Nike Master Trainer Traci Copeland," Thrive Global (February 18, 2020), https://thriveglobal.com/stories/traci-copeland-nike-trainer-reach-nutrition-movement-goals/.

68 **Luke Milton:** Lindsey Benoit O'Connell, "How to Use Friendship to Reach Your Fitness Goals," Thrive Global (December 18, 2019), https://thriveglobal.com/stories/resolutions-movement-fitness-workout-friends-goals/.

68 **Boris Kodjoe:** Lindsey Benoit O'Connell, "Spotlight on Actor and Fitness Expert Boris Kodjoe," Thrive Global (August 20, 2019), https://thriveglobal.com/stories/actor-boris-kodjoe-morning-workout-healthy-family-fitness/.

69 **makes our heart stronger:** Rachel Palekar, "Simple Exercises That Can Help Your Body, Mind, and Heart," Thrive Global (July 5, 2017), https://thriveglobal.com/stories/simple-exercises-that-can-help-your-body-mind-and-heart/.

69 **lowers our risk of diabetes:** American Diabetes Association Staff, "Get Smart About Risks and Diabetes Prevention,"

American Diabetes Association (2020), http://www.diabetes
.org/diabetes-risk/prevention.

69 **decreases stress levels:** Michal Stawicki, "6 of the Best (and
Quick) Methods to Relieve Stress," Thrive Global/The Lad-
ders (February 12, 2019), https://thriveglobal.com/stories
/quick-excercises-stress-reduction/.

69 **"sweat unity":** Ashley Camuso, "8 Ways to Help Your Fitness
Resolutions Stick," Thrive Global (December 20, 2019),
https://thriveglobal.com/stories/8-ways-to-help-your-fitness
-resolutions-stick/.

69 **data from 1.2 million people in the United States:** Sammi R.
Chekroud, Ralitza Gueorguieva, Amanda B. Zheutlin, Martin
Paulus, Harlan M. Krumholz, John H. Krystal, and Adam M.
Chekroud, "Association Between Physical Exercise and Mental Health in 1.2 Million Individuals in the USA Between
2011 and 2015: A Cross-Sectional Study," *The Lancet Psychiatry* 5, no. 9 (September 1, 2018): 739–746, https://doi.org
/10.1016/S2215-0366(18)30227-X.

69 **importance of having social support:** Joan Kaufman, Bao-
Zhu Yang, Heather Douglas-Palumberi, Shadi Houshyar,
Deborah Lipschitz, John H. Krystal, and Joel Gelernter, "Social Supports and Serotonin Transporter Gene Moderate Depression in Maltreated Children," *Proceedings of the National
Academy of Sciences* 101, no. 49 (December 7, 2004): 17316–
17321, https://doi.org/10.1073/pnas.0404376101.

70 **One in four people:** Emily N. Ussery, Janet E. Fulton, Deborah A. Galuska, Peter T. Katzmarzyk, and Susan A. Carlson,
"Joint Prevalence of Sitting Time and Leisure-Time Physical
Activity Among US Adults, 2015–2016," *Journal of the American Medical Association* 302, no. 19 (2018): 2036–2038, https://
jamanetwork.com/journals/jama/fullarticle/2715582.

70 **extended sitting:** Susan C. Gilchrist, Virginia J. Howard, Tomi
Akinyemiju, Suzanne E. Judd, Mary Cushman, Steven P.
Hooker, and Keith M. Diaz, "Association of Sedentary Behav-

ior with Cancer Mortality in Middle-Aged and Older US Adults," *Journal of the American Medical Association Oncology* 6, no. 8 (2020): 1210–1217, https://jamanetwork.com/journals /jamaoncology/article-abstract/2767093.

70   **James Levine, a professor of medicine at the Mayo Clinic:** Mary Macvean, "'Get Up!' or Lose Hours of Your Life Every Day, Scientist Says," *Los Angeles Times*, July 31, 2014, https:// www.latimes.com/science/sciencenow/la-sci-sn-get-up-2014 0731-story.html.

70   **reduce the harmful effects of what some experts call the sitting disease:** Sharon Reynolds, "Light Activity May Lower Harmful Effects of Sitting," *N.I.H. Research Matters*, February 5, 2019, https://www.nih.gov/news-events/nih-research -matters/light-activity-may-lower-harmful-effects-sitting.

70   **microbursts of activity:** Audrey Bergouignan, Kristina T. Legget, Nathan De Jong, Elizabeth Kealey, Janet Nikolovski, Jack L. Groppel, Chris Jordan, Raphaela O'Day, James O. Hill, and Daniel H. Bessesen, "Effect of Frequent Interruptions of Prolonged Sitting on Self-Perceived Levels of Energy, Mood, Food Cravings, and Cognitive Function," *International Journal of Behavioral Nutrition and Physical Activity* 13, no. 113 (2016), https://doi.org/10.1186/s12966 -016-0437-z.

70   **releasing our breath:** Christophe André, "Proper Breathing Brings Better Health," *Scientific American*, January 15, 2019, https://www.scientificamerican.com/article/proper-breathing -brings-better-health/.

71   **give our body a break from work:** Rebecca Muller, "3 Unexpected Ways to Take a Break from Work," Thrive Global (March 26, 2019), https://thriveglobal.com/stories/unexpected -simple-ways-break-from-work-tips/.

71   **Hoda Kotb:** Stephanie Fairyington, "Hoda Kotb's Research-Backed Self-Care Routine Can Dramatically Improve Your Life," Thrive Global (November 9, 2018), https://thriveglobal

.com/stories/hoda-kotbs-research-backed-self-care-routine
-can-dramatically-improve-your-life/.

71   **Ryan Holmes:** Ryan Holmes, "Why It's Time We Paid Employees to Exercise at Work," LinkedIn (January 26, 2017), https://www.linkedin.com/pulse/why-its-time-we-paid
-employees-exercise-work-ryan-holmes/.

72   **Nora Minno:** Lindsey Benoit O'Connell, "How Rethinking Your Workouts Can Transform Your Physical Health," Thrive Global (February 14, 2020), https://thriveglobal.com/stories
/daily-burn-nora-minno-tips-rethink-recharge-workout
-fitness-health/.

73   **study of over forty thousand Canadians:** Nicholas A. Howell, Jack V. Tu, Rahim Moineddin, Anna Chu, and Gillian L. Booth, "Association Between Neighborhood Walkability and Predicted 10-Year Cardiovascular Disease Risk: The CAN-HEART (Cardiovascular Health in Ambulatory Care Research Team) Cohort," *Journal of the American Heart Association* 8 (2019), https://doi.org/10.1161/JAHA.119.013146.

73   **Dutch researchers, shows:** J. Maas et al., "Morbidity Is Related to a Green Living Environment," *Journal of Epidemiology and Community Health* 63, no. 12 (December 2009): 967–73, https://jech.bmj.com/content/63/12/967.

74   **I-Min Lee:** Allison Aubrey, "10,000 Steps a Day? How Many You Really Need to Boost Longevity," *NPR*, May 29, 2019, https://www.npr.org/sections/health-shots/2019/05/29
/727943418/do-you-really-need-10-000-steps-per-day.

74   **participants who took 4,000 steps in a day got a boost in longevity:** I-Min Lee, Eric J. Shiroma, Masamitsu Kamada, David R. Bassett, Charles E. Matthews, and Julie E. Buring, "Association of Step Volume and Intensity with All-Cause Mortality in Older Women," *JAMA Internal Medicine* 179, no. 8 (2019): 1105–1112, doi:10.1001/jamainternmed.2019
.0899.

74   **study led by University of Illinois researchers:** Michelle W. Voss, Ruchika S. Prakash, Kirk I. Erickson, Chandramallika Basak, Laura Chaddock, Jennifer S. Kim, Heloisa Alves, Susie Heo, Amanda N. Szabo, Siobhan M. White, Thomas R. Wójcicki, Emily L. Mailey, Neha Gothe, Erin A. Olson, Edward McAuley, and Arthur F. Kramer, "Plasticity of Brain Networks in a Randomized Intervention Trial of Exercise Training in Older Adults," *Frontiers in Aging Neuroscience* 2, no. 32 (2010), https://doi.org/10.3389/fnagi.2010.00032.

75   **Microstep Diary, Gregory Beyer:** Gregory Beyer, "I Tried a Quick Burst of Exercise Most Mornings for 32 Days and Here's What Happened," Thrive Global (November 5, 2019), https://thriveglobal.com/stories/quick-burst-exercise-morning-routine-diary/.

CHAPTER 5: FOCUS AND PRIORITIZATION

79   **only 39 percent of our day is spent doing task-specific work:** Michael Chui, James Manyika, Jacques Bughin, Richard Dobbs, Charles Roxburgh, Hugo Sarrazin, Geoffrey Sands, and Magdalena Westergren, "The Social Economy: Unlocking Value and Productivity Through Social Technologies," McKinsey Global Institute (July 1, 2012), https://www.mckinsey.com/industries/technology-media-and-telecommunications/our-insights/the-social-economy.

81   **Wanda Holland Greene:** Thrive Global Staff, "Wanda Holland Greene On Reclaiming Her Space and Sanity," Thrive Global (January 25, 2018), https://thriveglobal.com/stories/wanda-holland-greene-on-reclaiming-her-space-and-sanity-2/.

82   **productivity to drop:** Joshua S. Rubenstein, David E. Meyer, and Jeffrey E. Evans, "Executive Control of Cognitive Processes in Task Switching," *Journal of Experimental Psychology:*

Human Perception and Performance 27, no. 4 (2001): 763–797, https://www.apa.org/pubs/journals/releases/xhp274763.pdf.

82   **David Strayer:** Maria Konnikova, "Multitask Masters," *New Yorker* (May 7, 2014), https://www.newyorker.com/science /maria-konnikova/multitask-masters.

82   **Valerie Wong Fountain:** Valerie Wong Fountain, "The Small Habit That Helps Valerie Wong Fountain Stay Productive and Organized," Thrive Global (May 5, 2020), https://thriveglobal .com/stories/valerie-wong-fountain-small-habit -productivity-tip-gold-house-questionnaire/.

82   **interrupted work:** Gloria Mark, Daniela Gudith, and Ulrich Klocke, "The Cost of Interrupted Work: More Speed and Stress," Proceedings of the 2008 Conference on Human Factors in Computing Systems (April 2008), 107–110, https://dl .acm.org/doi/10.1145/1357054.1357072.

82   **"toggle between tasks":** Mayo Oshin, "9 Ways Multitasking Is Killing Your Brain and Productivity, According to Neuroscientists," Thrive Global (October 15, 2018), https://thrive global.com/stories/9-ways-multitasking-is-killing-your -brain-and-productivity-according-to-neuroscientists/.

83   **James Clear:** Alex Dempsey, "James Clear: On Reclaiming His Attention to Focus on What Matters," Thrive Global (October 16, 2019), https://thriveglobal.com/stories/james-clear -on-reclaiming-his-attention-to-focus-on-what-matters/.

84   **Howard Weiss:** Thrive Global Staff, "How a Top Psychologist Tackles Prioritization," Thrive Global (December 11, 2017), https://thriveglobal.com/stories/how-a-top-psychologist -tackles-prioritization/.

84   **28 percent of the average workday:** Jonathan B. Spira and Joshua B. Feintuch, "The Cost of Not Paying Attention: How Interruptions Impact Knowledge Worker Productivity," Basex, Inc. (2004), http://www.brigidschulte.com/wp-content /uploads/2014/02/costofnotpayingattention.basexreport-2 .pdf.

85   **Jen Fisher:** Jen Fisher, "The Powerful Advice Jen Fisher Wants Women to Know About Preventing Burnout," Thrive Global (March 4, 2020), https://thriveglobal.com/stories/jen-fisher -well-being-advice-women-prevent-burnout/.

85   **shrink our brains:** Kep Kee Loh and Ryota Kanai, "Higher Media Multi-Tasking Activity Is Associated with Smaller Gray-Matter Density in the Anterior Cingulate Cortex," *PLoS ONE* 9, no. 9 (2014): e106698, doi: 10.1371/journal.pone.010 6698.

85   **University of Essex:** Andrew K. Przybylski and Netta Weinstein, "Can You Connect with Me Now? How the Presence of Mobile Communication Technology Influences Face-to-Face Conversation Quality," *Journal of Social and Personal Relationships* 30, no. 3 (2012): 237–246, https://journals.sagepub.com /doi/pdf/10.1177/0265407512453827?mod=article_inline.

86   **Roman philosopher Seneca:** Maria Popova, "The Shortness of Life: Seneca on Busyness and the Art of Living Wide Rather Than Living Long," Brainpickings, n.d., https://www .brainpickings.org/2014/09/01/seneca-on-the-shortness -of-life/.

87   **Shira Miller:** Shira Miller, "3 Ways That Slowing Down Can Actually Help You Get More Done," Thrive Global (December 31, 2018), https://thriveglobal.com/stories/learning-how -to-slow-down-accelerated-my-happiness-well-being-and -success/.

87   **Grace Byers:** Lindsey Benoit O'Connell, "Empire's Grace Byers Helps You to Focus and Feel Confident," Thrive Global (April 22, 2020), https://thriveglobal.com/stories/empires -grace-byers-helps-you-to-focus-and-feel-confident/.

88   **Richard Branson:** Catherine Clifford, "You Don't Have to Get Up Super Early to Be Successful. Just Ask Billionaires Warren Buffet and Elon Musk," CNBC.com (July 6, 2017), https://www.cnbc.com/2017/07/06/you-dont-have-to-wake -up-early-to-be-successful.html.

89 **Oprah:** Alexandra King, "'Stay in the Light': Oprah's Advice in an Age of Political Unrest," CNN.com (March 9, 2018), https://www.cnn.com/2018/03/09/us/oprah-stay-in-the -light-cnntv/index.html?sr=fbCNN031118oprah-stay -in-the-light-cnntv0344PMVODtop.

89 **prior level of focus:** Gloria Mark, Victor M. Gonzalez, and Justin Harris, "No Task Left Behind? Examining the Nature of Fragmented Work," University of California, Irvine, *CHI 2005* (April 2–7, 2005), https://www.ics.uci.edu/~gmark/CHI 2005.pdf.

90 **Leo Wong:** Leo Wong, "The Powerful Lesson Leo Wong Learned from a Major Turning Point in His Life," Thrive Global (May 4, 2020), https://thriveglobal.com/stories/leo -wong-life-lesson-turning-point-questioonnaire-gold-house/.

90 **Thomas Oppong:** Thomas Oppong, "The Distracted Mind (How to Increase Your Attention Span)," Thrive Global (February 28, 2019), https://thriveglobal.com/stories/boosting -attention-span-tips/.

92 **Mary Oliver:** Mary Oliver, "Yes! No!" *White Pine: Poems and Prose Poems* (San Diego: Harcourt Inc., 2014), 8.

92 **"how someone's mind works":** Tristan Harris, "How a Hand-ful of Tech Companies Control Billions of Minds Every Day," TED 2017 (April 2017), https://www.ted.com/talks/tristan _harris_how_a_handful_of_tech_companies_control_billions _of_minds_every_day/transcript.

92 **"shaping the menus":** Tristan Harris, "How Technology Is Hijacking Your Mind—from a Magician and Google Design Ethicist," Thrive Global (May 18, 2016), https://thriveglobal .com/stories/how-technology-is-hijacking-your-mind-from -a-magician-and-google-design-ethicist/.

92 **"helps our mind get back control of itself":** Tristan Harris, "What Your Notifications Do to Your Brain, and What to Do About It," Thrive Global (January 25, 2018), https://thrive

global.com/stories/what-your-notifications-do-to-your-brain-and-what-to-do-about-it-2/.

93 **Marcus Aurelius:** Marcus Aurelius, *Meditations*, trans. Gregory Hays (New York: Modern Library, 2012), Kindle edition.

94 **Nili Lotan:** Nili Lotan, "How Nili Lotan Reframes Negative Thinking in an Instant," Thrive Global (June 24, 2020), https://thriveglobal.com/stories/nili-lotan-reframes-negative-thinking-tip-family-work/.

94 **2015 Adobe report:** Kristin Naragon, "Subject: Email, We Just Can't Get Enough," *Adobe Blog* (August 26, 2015), https://blog.adobe.com/en/publish/2015/08/26/email.html#gs.i73u5h.

94 **Ashton Kutcher:** Kelsey Murray, "Ashton Kutcher's Simple yet Brilliant Email Strategy," Thrive Global (October 16, 2017), https://thriveglobal.com/stories/ashton-kutcher-s-simple-yet-brilliant-email-strategy/.

96 **Arianna found when she did a "life audit":** Arianna Huffington, *Thrive: The Third Metric to Redefining Success and Creating a Life of Well-Being, Wisdom, and Wonder* (New York: Harmony, 2014), 155.

96 **Tim Ferriss:** Robert Glazer, "To Be Successful You Need to Say No Often—Tim Ferriss Discovered the Formula That Works," Thrive Global (July 1, 2019), https://thriveglobal.com/stories/success-say-no-often-tim-ferriss-productivity-career/.

97 **A 2018 study:** "Effects of Physical Exercise on Cognitive Functioning and Wellbeing: Biological and Psychological Benefits," *Frontiers in Psychology* (2018), https://www.frontiersin.org/articles/10.3389/fpsyg.2018.00509.

97 **Blaise Pascal:** Adam Wernick, "A New Study Found People Are Terrible at Sitting Alone with Their Thoughts. How About You?," World (July 19, 2014), https://www.pri.org/stories/2014-07-19/new-study-found-people-are-terrible-sitting-alone-their-thoughts-how-about-you.

97   **meditators indeed experience less mind wandering:** Judson A. Brewer, Patrick D. Worhunsky, Jeremy R. Gray, Yi-Yuan Tang, Jochen Weber, and Hedy Kober, "Meditation Experience Is Associated with Differences in Default Mode Network Activity and Connectivity," *Proceedings of the National Academy of Sciences* 108, no. 50 (December 13, 2011): 20254–20259, https://doi.org/10.1073/pnas.1112029108.

97   **memory and storing information:** Imke Kirste, Zeina Nicola, Golo Kronenberg, Tara L. Walker, Robert C. Liu, and Gerd Kempermann, "Is Silence Golden? Effects of Auditory Stimuli and Their Absence on Adult Hippocampal Neurogenesis," *Brain Structure and Function* 220, no. 2 (December 2013): 1221–1228, 10.1007/s00429-013-0679-3.

97   **Giuseppe Pagnoni:** Giuseppe Pagnoni, Milos Cekic, and Ying Guo, "Thinking About Not-Thinking: Neural Correlates of Conceptual Processing During Zen Meditation," *PLoS ONE* 3, no. 9 (2008): e3083, https://journals.plos.org/plosone/article?id=10.1371/journal.pone.0003083.

97   **"The regular practice of meditation":** Charles Q. Choi, "Study: Zen Meditation Really Does Clear the Mind," Live Science, September 2, 2008, https://www.livescience.com/2829-study-zen-meditation-clear-mind.html.

98   **Microstep Diary, Kirsten Harman:** Kirsten Harman, "I Tried Meditating First Thing in the Morning Instead of Checking Social Media for 32 Days and Here's What Happened," Thrive Global (November 6, 2019), https://thriveglobal.com/stories/meditation-microstep-morning-ritual-social-media-diary/.

CHAPTER 6: COMMUNICATION AND RELATIONSHIPS

105   **Robert Waldinger:** Robert Waldinger, "What Makes a Good Life? Lessons from the Longest Study on Happiness," TED, n.d., https://www.ted.com/talks/robert_waldinger_what

_makes_a_good_life_lessons_from_the_longest_study_on
_happiness/transcript.

105 **heart disease and stroke:** Nicole K. Valtorta, Mona Kanaan, Simon Gilbody, Sara Ronzi, and Barbara Hanratty, "Loneliness and Social Isolation as Risk Factors for Coronary Heart Disease and Stroke: Systematic Review and Meta-Analysis of Longitudinal Observational Studies," *Heart* 102, no. 12 (2016), http://dx.doi.org/10.1136/heartjnl-2015-308790.

105 **depression:** Archana Singh and Nishi Misra, "Loneliness, Depression and Sociability in Old Age," *Industrial Psychiatry Journal* 18, no. 1 (2009): 51–55, https://www.ncbi.nlm.nih.gov/pmc/articles/PMC3016701/.

105 **increased mortality:** Julianne Holt-Lunstad, Timothy B. Smith, Mark Baker, Tyler Harris, and David Stephenson, "Loneliness and Social Isolation as Risk Factors for Mortality: A Meta-Analytic Review," *Perspectives on Psychological Science* 10, no. 2 (2015), https://doi.org/10.1177/1745691614568352.

105 **Mary Dillon:** Mary Dillon, "The Thrive Global Questionnaire with Mary Dillon," Thrive Global (June 19, 2019), https://thriveglobal.com/stories/the-thrive-questionnaire-with-mary-dillon/.

105 **Aristotle, for instance:** Aristotle, *The Nicomachean Ethics*, trans. David Ross (Oxford: Oxford University Press, 2009).

106 **Cicero:** Philip Freeman, "How to Be a Good Friend, According to an Ancient Philosopher," *Time* (October 9, 2019), https://time.com/5361671/how-to-be-a-friend-cicero/.

107 **Kimberly Perry:** Linsey Benoit O'Connell, "The Band Perry's Kimberly Perry on What It Means to Live a Good Life," Thrive Global (September 27, 2019), https://thriveglobal.com/stories/kimberly-perry-the-band-perry-relationships-heartbreak-rebuilding/.

107 **As Murthy writes:** Vivek H. Murthy, "Why Workplace Friendships Are More Important Even Outside of the Office,"

Thrive Global (April 28, 2020), https://thriveglobal.com /stories/work-friendships-workplace-office-productivity -connection/.

108   **John Gottman:** John Gottman, Julie Gottman, Doug Abrams, and Rachel Carlton Abrams, "We've Been Studying Couples for 40 Years—Here's What We Learned About Improving Your Odds of Lasting Love," Thrive Global (February 12, 2019), https://thriveglobal.com/stories/couples-relationship -therapists-lasting-love-advice/.

108   **As Marcus Aurelius advised:** Mark Forstater, *The Spiritual Teachings of Marcus Aurelius* (New York: Perennial, 2000).

109   **Matthew Siedhoff:** Matthew Siedhoff, "5 Microsteps That Have Improved My Well-Being This Year," Thrive Global (November 4, 2019), https://thriveglobal.com/stories/micro steps-that-have-improved-my-well-being-this-year/.

109   **University of Virginia's National Marriage Project:** Tara Parker-Pope, "The Generous Marriage," *New York Times* (December 8, 2011), https://well.blogs.nytimes.com/2011/12/08 /is-generosity-better-than-sex/.

109   **self-expanding activities:** A. Muise, C. Harasymchuk, L. C. Day, C. Bacev-Giles, J. Gere, and E. A. Impett, "Broadening Your Horizons: Self-Expanding Activities Promote Desire and Satisfaction in Established Romantic Relationships," *Journal of Personality and Social Psychology* 116, no. 2 (2019): 237–258, https://doi.org/10.1037/pspi0000148.

110   **"spark some of the feelings of desire":** Christian Jarrett, "Try Something New Together—Research Shows Engaging in 'Self-Expanding Activities' Rekindles the Sexual Desire of Long-Term Couples," *Research Digest: The British Psychological Society* (February 24, 2019), https://digest.bps.org.uk/2019 /02/14/try-something-new-together-research-shows -engaging-in-self-expanding-activities-rekindles-the-sexual -desire-of-long-term-couples/.

110   **Zeno of Citium:** Gordon Marino, "Are You Listening?," *New York Times* (December 17, 2019), https://www.nytimes.com /2019/12/17/opinion/art-of-listening.html.

110   **Active listening:** Carl R. Rogers and Richard E. Farson, *Active Listening* (Chicago: University of Chicago, 1957).

110   **Joe-Annis Iodice:** Alexandra Hayes Robinson, "Want to Be a Better Listener? Ask Someone Whose Job It Is (and No, We Don't Mean Therapists)," Thrive Global (February 7, 2019), https://thriveglobal.com/stories/how-to-be-better-listener -bartender-doctor-driver-teacher/.

111   **Jenny TeGrotenhuis:** The Gottman Institute, "13 Underrated Tips That Will Improve Your Relationship," Thrive Global (January 8, 2019), https://thriveglobal.com/stories/small -changes-better-relationship-expert-tips-close-connected/.

111   ***International Journal of Listening:*** Harry Weger Jr., Gina Castle Bell, Elizabeth M. Minei, and Melissa C. Robinson, "The Relative Effectiveness of Active Listening in Initial Interactions," *International Journal of Listening* 28 (2014): 13–31, https://doi.org/10.1080/10904018.2013.813234.

112   **a technique pioneered by Carl Rogers:** Courtney E. Ackerman, "10 Person-Centered Therapy Techniques Inspired by Carl Rogers," PositivePsychology.com (January 9, 2020), https://positivepsychology.com/client-centered-therapy/.

112   **Vernā Myers:** Vernā Myers, "Thriving Across Our Differences," Webinar, Thrive Global, 2020.

112   **Tess Jonas:** Alexandra Hayes Robinson, "Want to Be a Better Listener? Ask Someone Whose Job It Is (and No, We Don't Mean Therapists)," Thrive Global (February 7, 2019), https:// thriveglobal.com/stories/how-to-be-better-listener -bartender-doctor-driver-teacher/.

113   **mere presence of a phone nearby:** Adrian F. Ward, Kristen Duke, Ayelet Gneezy, and Maarten W. Bos, "Brain Drain: The Mere Presence of One's Own Smartphone Reduces

Available Cognitive Capacity," *Journal of the Association for Consumer Research* 2, no. 2 (April 2017), https://www.journals.uchicago.edu/doi/abs/10.1086/691462.

113 **John Gottman:** John Gottman, Julie Gottman, Doug Abrams, and Rachel Carlton Abrams, "We've Been Studying Couples for 40 Years—Here's What We Learned About Improving Your Odds of Lasting Love," Thrive Global (February 12, 2019), https://thriveglobal.com/stories/couples-relationship -therapists-lasting-love-advice/.

114 **Kristin Behfar:** Mallory Stratton, "How Compassionate Directness Can Help Us Disagree Constructively at Work," Thrive Global (August 30, 2019), https://thriveglobal.com /stories/how-disagree-work-problem-solve-debate-argue -compassionate-directness/.

114 **Kristin Behfar:** Thrive Global, "The Right Way to Vent Without Increasing Your Stress Levels," Thrive Global (August 22, 2019), https://thriveglobal.in/stories/the-right-way-to-vent -without-increasing-your-stress-levels/.

114 **Eve Rodsky:** Alexandra Hayes Robinson, "One Mom's Mission to Bring 'Fair Play' to the Home and the Office—Through a Card Game," Thrive Global (October 14, 2019), https:// thriveglobal.com/stories/eve-rodsky-fair-play-workplace -self-care/.

115 **Angela Santomero:** Lindsey Benoit O'Connell, "Blues Clues Creator Angela Santomero Explains What a Good Role Model for Children Really Looks Like," Thrive Global (November 19, 2019), https://thriveglobal.com/stories/angela -santomero-blues-clues-role-model-radical-kindness-positive -parenting/.

115 **An effective apology:** Stephanie Fairyington, "Apologizing Is Not As Simple As Saying 'Sorry'—Here's How to Make One Meaningful," Thrive Global (March 20, 2019), https://thrive global.com/stories/apologizing-is-not-as-simple-as-saying -sorry-heres-how-to-make-one-meaningful/.

116 **Greg Lutze:** Ashley Camuso, "The Co-Founder of VSCO Explains Why He Craved a Social Media App Free from Likes, Comments, and Ads," Thrive Global (December 11, 2019), https://thriveglobal.com/stories/greg-lutze-vsco-founder -social-media-community-photo-sharing/.

116 **"perpetual problems":** Jennifer Scott, "Managing Conflict: Solvable vs. Perpetual Problems," The Gottman Institute (July 2, 2012), https://www.gottman.com/blog/managing -conflict-solvable-vs-perpetual-problems/.

117 **Seneca:** "Keeping Your Cool: 40 Stoic Quotes on Taming Anger," Daily Stoic, n.d., https://dailystoic.com/keeping-your -cool-40-stoic-quotes-on-taming-anger/.

118 **Teri Hatcher:** Teri Hatcher, "Actress Teri Hatcher on How She Discusses Failure with Her Daughter," Thrive Global (January 25, 2018), https://thriveglobal.com/stories/teri/.

118 **"weak ties":** Mark S. Granovetter, "The Strength of Weak Ties," *American Journal of Sociology* 78, no. 6 (May 1973): 1360–1380, https://www.jstor.org/stable/2776392?seq=1.

118 **low-stakes relationships:** Allie Volpe, "Why You Need a Network of Low-Stakes, Casual Friendships," *New York Times* (May 6, 2019), https://www.nytimes.com/2019/05/06 /smarter-living/why-you-need-a-network-of-low-stakes -casual-friendships.html.

118 **the more weak ties a person has:** Gillian M. Sandstrom and Elizabeth W. Dunn, "Social Interactions and Well-Being: The Surprising Power of Weak Ties," *Personality and Social Psychology Bulletin* 40, no. 7 (2014), https://doi.org/10.1177/0146 167214529799.

118 **can even improve physical health:** "Interacting with More People Is Shown to Keep Older Adults More Active," UT News press release (February 20, 2019), https://news.utexas .edu/2019/02/20/interacting-with-more-people-is-shown -to-keep-older-adults-more-active/.

119 **Julianne Holt-Lunstad:** Thrive Global Staff, "A Q&A with Julianne Holt-Lunstad, PhD, Professor of Psychology and Neuroscience at Brigham Young University," Thrive Global (August 10, 2017), https://thriveglobal.com/stories/learning-to-improve-our-social-connections/.

119 **"high levels of what sociologists call integration":** Jennifer Breheny Wallace, "How Casual Daily Interactions Protect Your Health," *Washington Post* (July 7, 2018), https://www.washingtonpost.com/national/health-science/how-casual-daily-interactions-protect-your-health/2018/07/06/fc62a468-4e33-11e8-84a0-458a1aa9ac0a_story.html.

120 **Tal Ben-Shahar:** Tal Ben-Shahar, "How I Learned to Stop Waiting to Live My Life," Thrive Global (December 18, 2018), https://thriveglobal.com/stories/how-i-learned-to-stop-waiting-to-live/.

120 **forty-three hours per week:** "Average Hours Employed People Spent Working on Days Worked by Day of Week," US Bureau of Labor Statistics, news release, n.d., https://www.bls.gov/charts/american-time-use/emp-by-ftpt-job-edu-h.htm.

120 **recommended six hours per day:** Jennifer Robison, "The Business Case for Well-Being," Gallup (June 9, 2010), https://news.gallup.com/businessjournal/139373/Business-Case-Wellbeing.aspx.

121 **having a best friend at work:** Tom Rath and Jim Harter, "Your Friends and Your Social Well-Being," Gallup (August 19, 2010), https://news.gallup.com/businessjournal/127043/friends-social-wellbeing.aspx.

121 **can also increase our happiness:** Beth Azar, "Friends and Co-Workers," *American Psychological Association*, gradPSYCH (2012), https://www.apa.org/gradpsych/2012/01/relationships.

121 **foster a sense of community:** Rebecca Muller, "Here's How to Find Community in Your Everyday Life, Even if You're an Introvert," Thrive Global (March 13, 2019), https://thrive

global.com/stories/find-build-community-everyday-life
-connection/.

121 **seven times as likely:** Tom Rath and Jim Harter, "Your Friends
and Your Social Well-Being," Gallup (August 19, 2010),
https://news.gallup.com/businessjournal/127043/friends
-social-wellbeing.aspx.

121 **higher levels of retention:** Emma Seppälä and Marissa King,
"Having Work Friends Can Be Tricky, but It's Worth It,"
Harvard Business Review (August 8, 2017), https://hbr
.org/2017/08/having-work-friends-can-be-tricky-but-its
-worth-it.

121 **70 percent less likely to report burnout:** "Build an Exit Program That Improves Retention and Creates Positive Exit Experiences," Gallup, https://www.gallup.com/workplace/246
512/exit-perspective-paper.aspx.

124 **a live exchange is thirty-four times more likely:** M. Mahdi
Roghanizad and Vanessa K. Bohns, "Ask in Person: You're
Less Persuasive Than You Think over Email," *Journal of Experimental Social Psychology* 69 (March 2017): 223–226, https://
www.sciencedirect.com/science/article/abs/pii/S00221031163
0292X.

124 **Jeremy Berman:** Marina Khidekel, "5 Meaningful Examples
of Emotional Intelligence at Work," Thrive Global (June 21,
2019), https://thriveglobal.com/stories/emotional-intelligence
-examples-workplace-employee-success-compassionate
-directness/.

126 **Microstep Diary, Summer Mattice:** Summer Mattice, "I
Tried Journaling Every Night for 32 Days and Here's What
Happened," Thrive Global (November 5, 2019), https://
thriveglobal.com/stories/microstep-month-diary-journaling
-for-32-days/.

134 **Elaine Goldsmith-Thomas, film producer:** Elaine Goldsmith-Thomas, "What Gives Me Optimism: Film Producer Elaine Goldsmith-Thomas," Thrive Global (February 25, 2019), https://thriveglobal.com/stories/what-gives-me-optimism-elaine-goldsmith-thomas/.

135 **Richard Branson:** Thrive Global Staff, "The Book That Changed Richard Branson's Life," Thrive Global (January 28, 2018), https://thriveglobal.com/stories/the-book-that-changed-richard-branson-s-life-2/.

136 **Toni Ko:** Ashley Camuso, "NYX Cosmetics Founder Toni Ko Shares the Mindset Shifts That Lead to a Thriving Life," Thrive Global (December 20, 2019), https://thriveglobal.com/stories/nyx-cosmetics-founder-toni-ko-pets-make-us-better-business-leaders/.

136 **Walt Whitman:** Joel Myerson, *Whitman in His Own Time: A Biographical Chronicle of His Life, Drawn from Recollections, Memoirs, and Interviews by Friends and Associates* (Iowa City: University of Iowa Press, 1991), 35–36.

137 **Sherry Turkle:** Arianna Huffington, *Thrive: The Third Metric to Redefining Success and Creating a Life of Well-Being, Wisdom, and Wonder* (New York: Harmony, 2014), 180.

137 **the empty moments in our day, when our minds can disconnect and wander freely, boost creativity:** Guihyun Park, Beng-Chong Lim, and Hui Si Oh, "Why Being Bored Might Not Be a Bad Thing After All," *Academy of Management Discoveries* 5, no. 1 (March 2019): 78–92, https://doi.org/10.5465/amd.2017.0033.

138 **Sherry Turkle told Thrive:** Stephanie Fairyington, "Supercharge Your Creativity and Productivity By Doing . . . Nothing," Thrive Global (May 6, 2019), https://thriveglobal.com/stories/enhance-creativity-boredom-tips/.

138 **Bertrand Russell:** Bertrand Russell, *The Conquest of Happiness* (New York: H. Liveright, 1930).

139 **allow ourselves to daydream:** Christine A. Godwin, Michael A. Hunter, Matthew A. Bezdek, Gregory Lieberman, Seth Elkin-Frankston, Victoria L. Romero, Katie Witkiewitz, Vincent P. Clark, and Eric H. Schumacher, "Functional Connectivity Within and Between Intrinsic Brain Networks Correlates with Trait Mind Wandering," *Neuropsychologia* 103 (August 2017): 140–153, https://doi.org/10.1016/j.neuropsychologia.2017.07.006.

139 **unicorn space:** Eve Rodsky, "Living in Your Unicorn Space," *Fair Play: A Game-Changing Solution for when You Have Too Much to Do (and More Life to Live)* (New York: G. P. Putnam's Sons, 2019), 282–308.

140 *The Artist's Way*: Julia Cameron, *The Artist's Way: A Spiritual Path to Higher Creativity* (New York: Jeremy P. Tarcher/Putnam, 1992).

141 **Martin Lindstrom:** Martin Lindstrom, "Martin Lindstrom: 'The Smartphone Wave Kills Our Lives,'" Thrive Global (December 2, 2016), https://thriveglobal.com/stories/martin-lindstrom-the-smartphone-wave-kills-our-lives/.

141 **A survey of over 3,500 knitters:** Jill Riley, Betsan Corkhill, and Clare Morris, "The Benefits of Knitting for Personal and Social Wellbeing in Adulthood: Findings from an International Survey," *British Journal of Occupational Therapy* 76, no. 2 (2013): 50–57, https://doi.org/10.4276/030802213X13603244419077.

141 **other studies reinforce the connection between creative craft hobbies and enhanced well-being:** Emily L. Burt and Jacqueline Atkinson, "The Relationship Between Quilting and Wellbeing," *Journal of Public Health* 34, no. 1 (2012): 54–59, https://doi.org/10.1093/pubmed/fdr041.

141 **David Lynch:** David Lynch, *Catching the Big Fish: Meditation, Consciousness, and Creativity* (New York: TarcherPerigee, 2006).

142 **darkness or dim lighting:** Anna Steidle and Lioba Werth, "Freedom from Constraints: Darkness and Dim Illumination Promote Creativity," *Journal of Environmental Psychology* 35 (September 2013): 67–80, https://doi.org/10.1016/j.jenvp .2013.05.003.

142 **Jonathan Franzen:** Jonathan Franzen, "Jonathan Franzen's 10 Rules for Novelists," *Literary Hub* (November 15, 2018), https://lithub.com/jonathan-franzens-10-rules-for-novelists/.

142 **Zadie Smith:** Maria Popova, "'Make Sure You Read a Lot of Books': Writing Rules From Zadie Smith," *The Atlantic* (September 19, 2012), https://www.theatlantic.com/entertainment /archive/2012/09/make-sure-you-read-a-lot-of-books -writing-rules-from-zadie-smith/262581/.

143 **according to a Brazilian study:** Wilfredo Blanco, Catia M. Pereira, Vinicius R. Cota, Annie C. Souza, César Rennó-Costa, Sharlene Santos, Gabriella Dias, Ana M. G. Guerreiro, Adriano B. L. Tort, Adrião D. Neto, and Sidarta Ribeiro, "Synaptic Homeostasis and Restructuring Across the Sleep-Wake Cycle," *PLOS Computational Biology* (May 2015), https://doi.org/10.1371/journal.pcbi.1004241.

143 **Arthur Koestler:** Arthur Koestler, *The Act of Creation* (New York: Macmillan, 1964).

143 **Marie Forleo:** Lindsey Benoit O'Connell, "Marie Forleo on How to Get Anything We Want," Thrive Global (October 2, 2019), https://thriveglobal.com/stories/marie-forleo-everything -is-figureoutable-life-coach-tips-achieve-goals/.

143 **Paul McCartney:** "Paul McCartney: I Wish I Could Spend More Time with My Mother," *Telegraph* (February 26, 2013), https://www.telegraph.co.uk/culture/music/the-beatles/989 6636/Paul-McCartney-I-wish-I-could-spend-more-time -with-my-mother.html.

143 **Many of Salvador Dalí's surrealist paintings:** Exhibition, Salvador Dalí: Hand Painted Dream Photographs Selections from the Permanent Collection, Dalí Museum, St. Petersburg, FL, September 1, 2003, through January 1, 2004.

143 **periodic table:** Maria Popova, "How Mendeleev Invented His Periodic Table in a Dream," Brain Pickings (February 8, 2016), https://www.brainpickings.org/2016/02/08/mendeleev-periodic-table-dream/.

143 **Google can be credited to dreams:** Larry Page, "Larry Page's University of Michigan Commencement Address," Google News, Speech, Ann Arbor, MI (May 2, 2009), https://googlepress.blogspot.com/2009/05/larry-pages-university-of-michigan.html.

144 **"Dreaming may be our most creative conscious state":** Don H. Hockenbury and Sandra E. Hockenbury, *Discovering Psychology*, 5th ed. (New York: Worth Publishers, 2011), 152.

144 **Julie Larson-Green:** Thrive Global Staff, "Microsoft Exec Julie Larson-Green on the Value of Reconsidering Your Approach," Thrive Global (January 28, 2018), https://thriveglobal.com/stories/microsoft-exec-julie-larson-green-on-the-value-of-reconsidering-your-approach-2/.

144 **Journaling about our dreams:** Denholm J. Aspy, "Is Dream Recall Underestimated by Retrospective Measures and Enhanced by Keeping a Logbook? An Empirical Investigation," *Consciousness and Cognition* 42 (May 2016): 181–203, https://doi.org/10.1016/j.concog.2016.03.015.

144 **dream recall was linked with greater creativity:** Mauricio Sierra-Siegert, Emma-Louise Jay, Claudia Florez, and Ana Esther Garcia, "Minding the Dreamer Within: An Experimental Study on the Effects of Enhanced Dream Recall on Creative Thinking," *Journal of Creative Behavior* 53, no. 1 (March 2019): 83–96, https://doi.org/10.1002/jocb.168.

144 **dreams researcher Kelly Bulkeley:** Kelly Bulkeley, "Keeping a Dream Journal," *Psychology Today* (May 27, 2017), https://

www.psychologytoday.com/us/blog/dreaming-in-the-digital
-age/201705/keeping-dream-journal.

145 **research from LinkedIn Learning:** Paul Petrone, "Why Creativity Is the Most Important Skill in the World," *LinkedIn Learning Blog* (February 7, 2019), https://www.linkedin.com /pulse/why-creativity-most-important-skill-world-paul -petrone.

145 **walking is shown to increase creativity by as much as 60 percent:** Marily Oppezzo and Daniel L. Schwartz, "Give Your Ideas Some Legs: The Positive Effect of Walking on Creative Thinking," *Journal of Experimental Psychology: Learning, Memory, and Cognition* 40, no. 4 (2014): 1142–1152, https://doi .apa.org/doiLanding?doi=10.1037%2Fa0036577.

145 **Ernest Hemingway:** Ernest Hemingway, *A Moveable Feast* (New York: Charles Scribner's & Sons, 1964).

145 **Friedrich Nietzsche went even further:** Friedrich Nietzsche, *Sämtliche Werke: kritische Studienausgabe in 15 Bänden / 6 Der Fall Wagner. Götzen-Dämmerung. Der Antichrist. Ecce home. Dionysos-Dithyramben. Nietzsche contra Wagner*, eds. Giorgio Colli and Mazzino Montinari (Munich: Deutscher Taschenbuch Verlag, 1988), 64.

146 **Einstein wrote that:** Arthur Koestler, *The Act of Creation* (London: Pan Books Ltd., 1964), 260.

147 **"experiences of awe":** Melanie Rudd, Kathleen D. Vohs and Jennifer Aaker, "Awe Expands People's Perception of Time, Alters Decision Making, and Enhances Well-Being," *Psychological Science* 23, no. 10 (August 10, 2012): 1130–1136, https://doi.org/10.1177/0956797612438731.

147 **Jerry Saltz:** Elisabeth Egan, "Yes, You Can Channel Your Stress into Creativity. Here's How," *New York Times* (March 26, 2020), https://www.nytimes.com/2020/03/26 /books/review/how-to-be-an-artist-jerry-saltz.html.

148 **Listening to music:** David B. Yaden, Scott Barry Kaufman, Elizabeth Hyde, Alice Chirico, Andrea Gaggioli, Jia Wei

Zhang, and Dacher Keltner, "The Development of the Awe Experience Scale (AWE-S): A Multifactorial Measure for a Complex Emotion," *Journal of Positive Psychology* 14, no. 4 (2019): 474–488, https://doi.org/10.1080/17439760.2018.14 84940.

148   **interpersonal awe:** Marianna Graziosi and David Yaden, "Interpersonal Awe: Exploring the Social Domain of Awe Elicitors," *Journal of Positive Psychology* (November 14, 2019), https://doi.org/10.1080/17439760.2019.1689422.

149   **Microstep Diary, Mallory Stratton:** Mallory Stratton, "I Set a Firm End to My Workday for 32 Days and Here's What Happened," Thrive Global (November 6, 2019), https://thriveglobal.com/stories/microstep-month-diary-leave-office-earlier-workday/.

CHAPTER 8: PURPOSE AND MEANING

153   **"It has never been easier to run away from ourselves":** Dan Nixon, "The Battle for Your Attention," Garrison Institute (July 19, 2018), https://www.garrisoninstitute.org/blog/tag/crisis-of-attention/.

153   **nine out of ten career professionals said they'd accept lower future earnings:** Shawn Achor, Andrew Reece, et al., "9 Out of 10 People Are Willing to Earn Less Money to Do More-Meaningful Work," *Harvard Business Review* (November 6, 2018), https://hbr.org/2018/11/9-out-of-10-people-are-willing-to-earn-less-money-to-do-more-meaningful-work.

154   **"live life as if everything is rigged in your favor":** "Quotable Quote," Goodreads, https://www.goodreads.com/quotes/727 5104-live-life-as-if-everything-is-rigged-in-your-favor.

155   **"To all of you who made it all that it was, I send a quarter century's worth of thanks":** Darcy Jacobsen, "6 Famous Thank You Letters: How to Say Thanks and Be Heard," Workhuman, n.d., https://www.workhuman.com/resources/globoforce-blog

/6-famous-thank-you-letters-how-to-say-thanks-and-be
-heard.

156 **Vinutha Narayan:** Vinutha Narayan, "How Giving Can Transform You," Thrive Global (September 10, 2019), https://thriveglobal.com/stories/how-giving-can-transform-you-2/.

156 **"gratitude is not only the greatest of virtues but the parent of all the others":** Marcus Tullius Cicero, BrainyQuote, https://www.brainyquote.com/quotes/marcus_tullius_cicero_122152.

156 **"Convince yourself that everything is the gift of the gods":** "Marcus Aurelius' Meditations: Are You Ever Going to Achieve Goodness?," *Simple Thing Called Life*, http://www.simplethingcalledlife.com/stcl/marcus-aurelius-soul-quote/.

157 **Epictetus said that every situation has two handles:** "What Do You See?," Daily Stoic, n.d., https://dailystoic.com/what-do-you-see/.

157 **One study from Indiana University found that practicing gratitude:** Y. Joel Wong, Jesse Owen, Nicole T. Gabana, Joshua W. Brown, Sydney McInnis, Paul Toth, and Lynn Gilman, "Does Gratitude Writing Improve the Mental Health of Psychotherapy Clients? Evidence from a Randomized Controlled Trial," *Psychotherapy Research* 28, no. 2 (2018): 192–202, doi: 10.1080/10503307.2016.1169332.

157 **Neuroplasticity (our brain's ability to constantly create new neural pathways):** Joseph Rauch, "Have You Heard of Neurocounseling?," Talkspace (May 5, 2016), https://www.talkspace.com/blog/have-you-heard-of-neurocounseling/.

158 **Dr. Martin Seligman, one of the founders of the field of positive psychology:** Martin E. P. Seligman and Tracy A. Steen, "Positive Psychology Progress: Empirical Validation of Interventions," *American Psychologist* 60, no. 5 (2005): 410–421, https://www.researchgate.net/publication/7701091_Positive_Psychology_Progress_Empirical_Validation_of_Interventions.

158   **Tiffany Shlain:** Lindsey Benoit O'Connell, "Waking Up Extra Early Helps This Entrepreneur Be More Productive at Work," Thrive Global (December 24, 2019), https://thrive global.com/stories/tiffany-shlain-filmmaker-webby-awards -productivity-destress/.

158   **"intentionally bringing into awareness the tiny, previously unnoticed elements of the day":** Danny Penman, *Mindfulness: An Eight-Week Plan for Finding Peace in a Frantic World* (New York: Rodale Books, 2012).

159   **Researchers at the John Templeton Foundation found that:** Emiliana R. Simon-Thomas and Jeremy Adam Smith, "How Grateful Are Americans?," *Greater Good Magazine* (January 10, 2013), https://greatergood.berkeley.edu/article/item /how_grateful_are_americans.

159   **It's a practice LEMS sneakers entrepreneur Andrew Rademacher does every day:** Lindsey Benoit O'Connell, "The Thrive Questionnaire with LEMS Founder Andrew Rademacher," Thrive Global (August 21, 2019), https://thrive global.com/stories/lems-founder-andrew-rademacher -startup-entreprenuer-prioritization-organization/.

159   **It can lower levels of stress and depression:** Alex M. Wood, John Maltby, Raphael Gillett, P. Alex Linley, and Stephen Joseph, "The Role of Gratitude in the Development of Social Support, Stress, and Depression: Two Longitudinal Studies," *Journal of Research in Personality* 42, no. 4 (2008): 854–871, https://www.sciencedirect.com/science/article/abs/pii /S0092656607001286?via%3Dihub.

159   **It can lower levels of stress and depression:** Nancy Digdon and Amy Koble, "Effects of Constructive Worry, Imagery Distraction, and Gratitude Interventions on Sleep Quality: A Pilot Trial," *Applied Psychology: Health and Well-Being* 3, no. 2 (2011): 193–206, doi: 10.1111/j.1758-0854.2011.01049.x.

159   **In adolescents, gratitude has been found to reduce materialism:** Lan Nguyen Chaplin, Deborah Roedder John, Aric

Rindfleisch, and Jeffrey J. Froh, "The Impact of Gratitude on Adolescent Materialism and Generosity," *Journal of Positive Psychology* 14, no. 4 (2019): 502–511, doi: 10.1080/17439 760.2018.1497688.

159 **even lead to healthier eating:** Megan M. Fritz, Christina N. Armenta, et al., "Gratitude Facilitates Healthy Eating Behavior in Adolescents and Young Adults," *Journal of Experimental Social Psychology* 81 (2019): 4–14, https://www.sciencedirect .com/science/article/abs/pii/S0022103117308569.

159 **At the other end of life, gratitude has been found to reduce loneliness:** Monica Y. Bartlett and Sarah N. Arpin, "Gratitude and Loneliness: Enhancing Health and Well-Being in Older Adults," *Research on Aging* 41, no. 8 (2019): 772–793, https://pubmed.ncbi.nlm.nih.gov/31043126/.

159 **"reflect upon your present blessings, of which every man has plenty":** "Charles Dickens Quotes," BrainyQuote, https:// www.brainyquote.com/quotes/charles_dickens_121978.

160 **"My heart is at ease knowing that what was meant for me":** "Quotable Quote," *Goodreads*, https://www.goodreads.com /quotes/812276-my-heart-is-at-ease-knowing-that-what -was-meant.

160 **JFK:** Jitske M. C. Both-Nwabuwe, Maria T. M. Dijkstra, and Bianca Beersma, "Sweeping the Floor or Putting a Man on the Moon: How to Define and Measure Meaningful Work," *Frontiers in Psychology* 8 (September 2017): 1658, https:// www.frontiersin.org/articles/10.3389/fpsyg.2017.01658/full.

161 **Karena Dawn:** Lindsey Benoit O'Connell, "The Tone It Up Girls Share How to Tap into Your Surroundings to Alleviate Stress," Thrive Global (October 21, 2019), https://thrive global.com/stories/tone-it-up-mental-health-alleviate-stress/.

162 **In a well-known study, Yale School of Management professor Amy Wrzesniewski:** David Zax, "Want to Be Happier at Work? Learn How from These 'Job Crafters,'" *Fast Company* (June 3, 2013), https://www.fastcompany.com/3011081

/want-to-be-happier-at-work-learn-how-from-these
-job-crafters.

162 **Wrzesniewski didn't interview doctors:** Amy Wrzesniewski
and Jane Dutton, "Having a Calling and Crafting a Job: The
Case of Candice Billups," William Davidson Institute at the
University of Michigan, 2009, https://wdi-publishing.com
/product/having-a-calling-and-crafting-a-job-video-the-case
-of-candice-billups/.

162 **"I have so much to offer sick people":** Jessica Amortegui, "The
Secret to More Meaningful Work," *Forbes* (November 17,
2015), https://www.forbes.com/sites/womensmedia/2015/11
/17/the-secret-to-more-meaningful-work/#4a8780a95116.

162 **In fact, a desire for more meaning and purpose is one of the
overarching trends:** "The Evolution of Work: The Changing
Nature of the Global Workplace," ADP Research Institute
(2016), https://www.adp.com/resources/articles-and-insights
/articles/t/the-evolution-of-work-the-changing-nature-of
-the-global-workplace.aspx.

163 **V. R. Ferose:** V. R. Ferose, "5 Ways to Help Find Your Purpose," Thrive Global (August 27, 2019), https://thriveglobal
.com/stories/how-to-find-your-purpose-life-wisdom/.

163 **According to a 2017 survey of over 2,000 workers by BetterUp:** Brian O'Connell, "The Search for Meaning," SHRM
(March 23, 2019), https://www.shrm.org/hr-today/news/all
-things-work/pages/the-search-for-meaning.aspx.

164 **Antoni Porowski:** Lindsey Benoit O'Connell, "Queer Eye's
Antoni Porowski Shares His Secret to Stress-Free Meal Prep,"
Thrive Global (September 12, 2019), https://thriveglobal.com
/stories/antoni-porowski-queer-eye-stress-free-cooking/.

164 **On the space theme once more, NASA cadet Alyssa Carson
has realized:** Ashley Camuso, "How the World's Youngest
Astronaut-in-Training Plans to Be on Mars by 2030," Thrive
Global (October 25, 2019), https://thriveglobal.com/stories
/alyssa-carson-nasa-astronaut-goals-determination/.

164   **Jen Fisher:** Jen Fisher, "The Thrive Guide to Rediscovering Your Purpose at Work," Thrive Global (October 14, 2019), https://thriveglobal.com/stories/rediscover-purpose-at-work/.

165   **musician and activist Lenny Kravitz's passion project:** Eiman Al Zaabi, "When Passion Meets Purpose," Thrive Global (May 12, 2017), https://thriveglobal.com/stories/when-passion-meets-purpose/.

166   **And former First Lady Michelle Obama has used her voice:** Emily C. Johnson, "11 Things I Learned from Attending Michelle Obama's Book Tour," Thrive Global (December 20, 2018), https://thriveglobal.com/stories/11-things-i-learned-from-attending-michelle-obamas-book-tour/.

166   **A fascinating study from the Wharton, Yale, and Harvard business schools:** Cassie Mogilner, Zoë Chance, and Michael I. Norton, "Giving Time Gives You Time," *Psychological Science* 23, no. 10 (2012): 1233–1238, https://journals.sagepub.com/doi/abs/10.1177/0956797612442551#article CitationDownloadContainer.

167   **As Mia Birdsong puts it:** Mia Birdsong, *How We Show Up: Reclaiming Family, Friendship, and Community* (New York: Hachette Books, 2020).

167   **Maria Menounos:** Lindsey Benoit O'Connell, "Maria Menounos: 'I'm on a Journey to Keep Getting Better,'" Thrive Global (October 16, 2019), https://thriveglobal.com/stories/maria-menounos-mental-health-morning-routine/.

167   **"A generous person will prosper; whoever refreshes others will be refreshed":** "Proverbs 11:25," Bible Hub, https://biblehub.com/proverbs/11-25.htm.

167   **"Through selfless service, you will always be fruitful":** "Chapter 3: Selfless Service," Global Cultures, n.d., http://www.globalcultures.net/asianstudies/Chapter%203-%20partial.htm.

168   **"There is more happiness in giving than there is in receiving":** "More Happiness in Giving," Watchtower Online

Library, n.d., https://wol.jw.org/en/wol/d/r1/lp-e/1971407 #h=3.

168 **"No one can live happily who has regard for himself"**: "Quotable Quote," Goodreads, https://www.goodreads.com/quotes /7628266-no-one-can-live-happily-who-has-regard-for -himself.

168 **"I have found that the only thing that does bring you happiness is doing"**: "David Letterman Quotes," BrainyQuote, https://www.brainyquote.com/quotes/david_letterman _608465.

168 **"I've been working a lot with the United Nations Refugee Agency"**: Alexandra Hayes Robinson, "Why Jillian Michaels Has Been Flexing Her Meditation Muscle," Thrive Global (October 10, 2019), https://thriveglobal.com/stories/mental -health-jillian-michaels-signs-stressors-steps/.

168 **One study found that volunteering at least once a week gives you**: Lara B. Aknin, Christopher P. Barrington-Leigh, et al., "Prosocial Spending and Well-Being: Cross-Cultural Evidence for a Psychological Universal," *Journal of Personality and Social Psychology* 104, no. 4 (2013): 635–652, https://www.apa .org/pubs/journals/releases/psp-104-4-635.pdf.

168 **In this study, researchers from Simon Fraser University:** Lara B. Aknin, Elizabeth W. Dunn, et al., "Does Social Connection Turn Good Deeds into Good Feelings?: On the Value of Putting the 'Social' in Prosocial Spending," *International Journal of Happiness and Development* (January 2013), https:// www.hbs.edu/faculty/Publication%20Files/aknin%20dunn %20sandstrom%20norton_ecebf8d6-171f-484e-b4b5-1939b f2b5d8c.pdf.

169 **"Since you get more joy out of giving joy to others"**: "Quotable Quote," Goodreads, https://www.goodreads.com/quotes /46578-since-you-get-more-joy-out-of-giving-joy-to.

170 **Victoria Arlen:** Lindsey Benoit O'Connell, "ESPN's Victoria Arlen Wants You to Take a Step Back and Breathe," Thrive

Global (October 11, 2019), https://thriveglobal.com/stories /espns-victoria-espn-mental-health-stress-solutions/.

170 **A Baylor University study found that people who pray to a loving God:** Christopher G. Ellison, Matt Bradshaw, et al., "Prayer, Attachment to God, and Symptoms of Anxiety-Related Disorders Among U.S. Adults," *Sociology of Religion* 75, no. 2 (2014): 208–233, http://www.baylorisr.org/wp -content/uploads/Sociology-of-Religion-2014-Ellison-208 -33.pdf.

170 **"It's amazing how simply stopping for a moment and trusting that you can":** Elaine Lipworth, "The Power of Prayer Can Guide Us Through This Challenging Time," Thrive Global (April 2, 2020), https://thriveglobal.com/stories/prayer-how -to-pray-power-connection-stay-positive-calm/.

171 **"In all Asian languages":** Jon Kabat-Zinn, *Arriving at Your Own Door: 108 Lessons in Mindfulness* (New York: Hyperion, 2007), 3.

172 **For singer Katy Perry, meditating for twenty minutes:** Kelsey Murray, "Katy Perry on Wake-Up Calls and the Importance of Prioritizing Mental Health," Thrive Global (August 14, 2017), https://thriveglobal.com/stories/katy-perry-on-wake-up -calls-and-the-importance-of-prioritizing-mental-health/.

172 **Melinda Gates makes it a habit too:** Thrive Global Staff, "Melinda Gates on the Invaluable Advice Her Mom Gave Her About Success as a Teenager," Thrive Global (January 25, 2018), https://thriveglobal.com/stories/melinda-gates-on-the -invaluable-advice-her-mom-gave-her-about-success-as-a -teenager-2/.

172 **"We don't always have 20 minutes to meditate":** Alexandra Hayes Robinson, "How Melinda Gates Recharges Her Mental Batteries in Less Than 5 Minutes," Thrive Global (October 10, 2019), https://thriveglobal.com/stories/mental-health -melinda-gates-stress-signs-steps-self-care/.

172   "further reaches of human plasticity": Richard Davidson, interview with Krista Tippett, *On Being with Krista Tippett*, American Public Media (June 23, 2011), https://onbeing.org /programs/richard-davidson-investigating-healthy-minds /#transcript.

172   "What we found is that the trained mind, or brain": Marc Kaufman, "Meditation Gives Brain a Charge, Study Finds," *Washington Post* (January 3, 2005), https://www.washington post.com/archive/politics/2005/01/03/meditation-gives -brain-a-charge-study-finds/7edabb07-a035-4b20-aebc-16f4 eac43a9e/.

172   "Meditation is not just blissing out under a mango tree": Arianna Huffington, "Meditation: It's Not Just for Enlightenment Anymore," Thrive Global (November 30, 2016), https:// thriveglobal.com/stories/meditation-it-s-not-just-for -enlightenment-anymore/.

173   According to Taoist philosophy: Bernard Down, "Death in Classical Daoist Thought," *Philosophy Now*, 2000, https:// philosophynow.org/issues/27/Death_in_Classical_Daoist _Thought.

173   Saint Benedict established the tradition of Lectio Divina ("divine reading"): "Lectio Divina: Divine Reading," E-Benedictine, https://e-benedictine.com/lectio-divina/.

174   "It is a time to choose what matters and what passes away": Renee Moorefield, "Filtering the Noise to Make the Best Choices," Global Wellness Institute (August 3, 2020), https:// globalwellnessinstitute.org/global-wellness-institute-blog /2020/06/11/august-filter/.

174   Bruce Feiler explores just how meaningful these moments: Bruce Feiler, *Life Is in the Transitions: Mastering Change at Any Age* (London: Penguin, 2020).

175   famous 1986 study by James Pennebaker of the University of Texas at Austin: Arianna Huffington, "Meditation: It's Not

Just for Enlightenment Anymore," Thrive Global (November 30, 2016), https://thriveglobal.com/stories/meditation-it -s-not-just-for-enlightenment-anymore/.

175   **famous 1986 study by James Pennebaker of the University of Texas at Austin:** J. W. Pennebaker and S. K. Beall, "Confronting a Traumatic Event: Toward an Understanding of Inhibition and Disease," *Journal of Abnormal Psychology* 95 (1986): 274–281, https://pubmed.ncbi.nlm.nih.gov/3745650/.

176   **"Intuition, not intellect, is the 'open sesame' of yourself":** "Quotable Quote," Goodreads, https://www.goodreads.com /quotes/7606666-intuition-not-intellect-is-the-open-sesame -of-yourself.

176   **"opinion, science, illumination":** "Quotable Quote," Goodreads, https://www.goodreads.com/quotes/9132911-knowledge -has-three-degrees—opinion-science-illumination-the-means.

176   **"that many important decisions are not arrived at by linear reasoning, but by intuition":** Martin E. P. Seligman and Michael Kahana, "Unpacking Intuition: A Conjecture," *Perspectives on Psychological Science* 4, no. 4 (2009): 399–402, https:// doi.org/10.1111/j.1745-6924.2009.01145.x.

177   **This was the place that Marcus Aurelius, the emperor of Rome for nineteen years:** Marcus Aurelius, *Meditations* (Mineola: Dover Publications, 1997).

179   **Microstep Diary, Kasia Laskowski:** Kasia Laskowski, "I Tried Journaling Every Day for a Month and Here's What I Learned," Thrive Global (January 10, 2019), https://thrive global.com/stories/journaling-microstep-month-diary -lessons/.

INDEX